What People Are Saying about
Peace to All Beings

"A valuable resource for those seeking to expand the circle of compassion to include all of our animal friends through spiritual meditation, prayer, and visualization."—**Elliot M. Katz, DVM**, President, In Defense of Animals

"This book belongs with Rev. Andrew Linzey's *Animal Rites* in providing believers in a suffering God with a texture of ideas that weave the earth and all of its creatures into an image of the world as it ought to be and, by the help of such books, may become."—**Karen Davis, Ph.D.**, President, United Poultry Concerns, Author, *Prisoned Chickens, Poisoned Eggs*

"This book offers spiritual guidance for those who have already travelled some distance along the path that integrates compassion for all beings into their daily lives and is an invaluable guide for those who are just beginning this journey."—**Rev. J.R. Hyland**, Editorial Director, *Humane Religion*, Author, *God's Covenant with Animals*

"*Peace to All Beings* is a book so full of inspiration and information that it could lead us toward our destiny of becoming *Homo ahimsa*—compassionate man."—**Louann Stahl**, Author, *A Most Surprising Song*

"A commendable workbook brimming with insights from visionaries such as Gandhi, Yogananda, Jane Goodall, and St. Francis of Assisi. *Peace to All Beings* is a synthesis of love, compassion, and reverence for all living beings. A book too important *not* to read."—**Edward Lee Amerson**, Author, *Sing with Wolves* and *On Silent Wings*

"When Judy Carman asks us in *Peace to All Beings* to protect the lives of all living creatures, is she asking us to join her in the impossible dream? Judging from the increasing number of people working to stop the abuse and killing of animals, such requests are not falling on deaf ears. I pray that *Peace to All Beings* will reach the hearts and souls of many, many readers."—**Bill Schul, Ph.D.**, Psychologist and Author, *Animal Immortality*

Peace to All Beings
Veggie Soup for the Chicken's Soul

JUDY CARMAN

To our brothers and sisters,
the animals of earth.
Together, let us create
a world of compassion
for all our children.

Lantern Books • New York
A Division of Booklight Inc.

2003
Lantern Books
One Union Square West, Suite 201
New York, NY 10003
Copyright Judy Carman, 2003

Printed in the United States of America

Library of Congress Cataloging-in-Publication Data

Carman, Judy McCoy.
Peace to all beings : veggie soup for the chicken's soul / Judy M. Carman.
p. cm.
Includes bibliographical references.
ISBN 1-59056-005-1 (alk. paper)
1. Animal welfare—Religious aspects. 2. Prayers for animals.
I. Title.
BL439.C37 2003
291.5'693—dc21
2003000420

printed on 100% post-consumer waste paper, chlorine-free

UNIVERSAL PEACE PRAYER FOR THE ANIMALS

Let us take a moment each day to
breathe deeply, close our eyes, visualize, and say:

*Compassion Encircles the Earth
for All Beings Everywhere.*

TABLE OF CONTENTS

Chapter Eight

FOREWORD

By Gene Bauston, M.P.S.
Co-founder and Director of Farm Sanctuary

HUMAN BEINGS HAVE LIVED AND EVOLVED TOGETHER
with the other animals for millennia. We have been
inspired and awed by them, and even deified them. But
we have also acted cruelly toward them, and today, our
exploitation of non-human animals has reached unpar-
alleled proportions. Nearly ten billion animals are
exploited and killed by the agribusiness industry every
year in the U.S. alone.

Tragically, most human cultures regard animals as
saleable commodities, property, and resources, rather
than as living, feeling beings with the same needs that
we have for affection, freedom, respect, and, indeed, for
life itself. As Judy points out in *Peace to All Beings*, millions of companion animals are mistreated and discarded; huge numbers of wild animals lose their homes to
human development and are killed by hunters, many to
the point of extinction; and factory farm animals die by

the billions at our hands. We control and manipulate
every aspect of the lives of farm animals, from concep-
tion to slaughter, in order to enhance their commercial
value. Such manipulation helps businesses to be profitable, but it also causes unimaginable animal suffering.

Modern dairy cows produce ten times more milk
than is normal. This puts severe strain on their bodies,
and they are commonly worn out and sent to slaughter
after just a few years of "production," even though they
could live over 25 years in a healthy environment.
Chickens now grow twice as fast as they normally
would due to genetic manipulation as well as artificial
stimulants. They often die of heart attacks at just a few
weeks of age since their hearts cannot support this
excessive growth rate and the stressful living conditions
to which they are subjected.

When we human beings commodify and mistreat
other animals, we violate their rights to peace and happiness, and we violate our own natural feelings of compassion. When we see other sentient beings merely as
commodities, we cannot be inspired by them. We fail to
see and understand them as beings in their own right,
and we fail to empathize with them. In order to deny
them their right to live, we have to refuse to look into
their eyes, just as witch killers refused to look into the
eyes of their human victims for fear of being moved to
compassion.

In order to kill animals, we force ourselves to see them as separate and different from ourselves, just as humans practicing violence against other humans must convince themselves that they are different and separate from their human victims.

But it is this illusion of separation that causes a great emptiness in our souls. We are intricately connected with the other animals, and we ourselves are harmed when we wage violence against them. We share much of the same genetic makeup and evolutionary development. We breathe the same air, drink the same water, and are sustained by the same earth and sun. By perpetrating cruelty against other animals, our hearts become hardened, and we become dead to much of Earth's beauty.

In *Peace to All Beings,* Judy Carman encourages us all to reconnect with our animal brothers and sisters and, in so doing, to reconnect with the deepest parts of ourselves. This is a timely and important book. It calls upon the wisdom of human teachers throughout the ages who have taught that the experience of true inner joy is found in the wondrous revelation that all life is connected and sacred. Kindness, compassion, and respect for both human and non-human life are necessary steps on the path to inner peace. *Peace to All Beings* gives much needed help and hope at this pivotal time on earth when we are being asked to create a world of love, compassion, and peace for us all.

Gene Bauston is the Co-founder and Director of Farm Sanctuary. He graduated with a M.P.S. degree in Agricultural Economics from Cornell University. Farm Sanctuary is a leading farm animal protection organization that operates sanctuaries for rescued farm animals in New York and California.

Gene has paid thousands of visits to farms, stockyards, and slaughterhouses, where he has documented animal abuse. National and international news coverage of his undercover filmed evidence has helped raise awareness of the plight of farm animals. He is the author of Battered Birds, Crated Herds: How We Treat the Animals We Eat. *To learn more about Farm Sanctuary, go to www.farmsanctuary.org or call (607) 583-2225.*

Introduction

Until we extend our circle of compassion to include all living things, we will not ourselves find peace.—Albert Schweitzer (paraphrased)[1]

This lightworkers' handbook is:

- *For those who wish to help free the chickens from the soup pots, the cows from the slaughterhouses, the mink from the fur farms, the wild animals from extinction, indeed, to free all animals from suffering and from their bondage to human beings, and, in so doing, to help free humanity from its bondage to violence.*

- *For all of you who long to help create a world blessed with peace and nonviolence.*

- *For all of you who walk a spiritual path, hold Love as your aim, and see the connection between your own inner peace and that of all others.*

- *For all of you who want to make a difference and to become the change you seek in the world.*
- *For all of you who love the earth and dedicate yourselves to the earth's healing.*
- *For everyone who desires the joy of inner peace.*
- *And for all the animals of earth who, though they cannot read this book, will nevertheless feel the impact of its visions and prayers and who are evolving along with us on this journey to the new consciousness of compassion.*

In this handbook you will find:

- *Why human wars and violence will not end until the war on animals ends. Reverence for all life is the missing piece to the puzzle of world peace, inner peace, and environmental healing and sustainability.*
- *That futurists, mystics, philosophers, and scientists declare that we are evolving to a higher level of consciousness at this time in our history and awakening to our destiny as non-violent, compassionate beings. We are actually evolving*

into new creatures. It's a bit like a caterpillar transforming into a butterfly or a seed transmuting into a tree. We are in a dark, earthy, chrysalis time. Violence seems to be exploding everywhere. But as we face today's challenges with faith in the Light up ahead, we find that we are coming out into the light as new creatures.

- *That as we evolve toward being more loving, we are enthusiastically assisted by the Divine Energy of the Universe. What is pulling us forward into this transformation? It is the magnetic force of Divine, Infinite, Unconditional Love. We are made of that Love, and we can utilize it to help bring harmony and healing to the earth and to all beings.*

- *That we have the power to change the world and make it better. We can utilize the phenomenal power of our own thoughts and intentions to create a compassionate, peaceful world. Whether you call it the power of thought or the power of prayer, it works to alter energy fields. We have the power within us to increase or*

> decrease the harmony in the energy
> fields of earth.
> * A collection of prayers, chants, posi-
>   tive thoughts, meditations, vows, and
>   visualizations to use for the animals
>   and for the healing and blessing of all
>   beings everywhere.

A Metaphysical Challenge

The plight of animals is a physical challenge that requires vigils, legislation, letters, education, boycotts, and rescues. It is also a metaphysical challenge, a challenge for all of us to search deeply within. To bring peace to the animals, we must be peace. We are being called to help bring love and compassion to all beings. Jane Goodall in her book *Reason for Hope* encourages us all to lend a hand and give of our hearts. She states, "We will have to evolve, all of us, from ordinary, everyday human beings—into saints."

This is a handbook for the new animal saints and lightworkers all over the world who are seeking to expand the circle of compassion to include all life. May it give you encouragement, peace, and strength for your journey, and belief in your own awesome power. You are an integral part of this dynamic shift in human consciousness.

Great spiritual teachers affirm that our inner spiritual power, peace, and joy increase to the degree that we let go of all acts and thoughts of cruelty or hostility for anyone, including all animals. The reason for that is simple. As we let go of anger and fear, we draw nearer to the Creator and to Love, and that brings rivers of joy to the soul and wings to the heart.

Animal Rights Are Human Rights

It has been said that injustice to animals is less important and should be ignored for now until hunger, racism, war, and human rights violations are eradicated.

There are three reasons why animal justice work must not be delayed:

- Those who are called to the work of animal rights have an intrinsic role in the Cosmic plan for peace on earth. Their calling cannot be judged less important or unimportant, since none of us can see the Bigger Plan. As we enter these new days of transformation, we must encourage each other to follow our own true nature.
- All those working for animal rights do so out of a powerful love in their hearts. Any work that channels more love energy into the world benefits everyone everywhere.
- Animal rights and human rights to dignity, respect, and compassion cannot be separated from each other. They are one and the same.

Whatever we do to the animals we do to ourselves. Whatever we do to end violence on any front, we do for the good of all.

This book is a call to end the alienation of animals and the animal advocacy movement from the mainstream of human life. Animal rights *are* human rights. Animal issues are peace, justice, and environmental issues. People who abuse or kill humans are nearly always abusive to animals. Human hunger is directly linked to excessive meat eating. For example, one acre of land can be dedicated either to producing 165 pounds of cow meat or 20,000 pounds of potatoes. Our water quality is suffering from the pollution produced by factory farms. The examples of the interconnections between justice and environmental and animal issues are endless.

We cannot save the world just for us. We are all connected. What we do to any being anywhere, we do to ourselves.

Waking Up Our Love

We are embarking together on the global awakening to higher consciousness. This is not our imagination. It is really happening. We are evolving, awakening to new heights of awareness. Jean Houston calls this "Jump Time." We are all poised to jump up to a new plateau of understanding about who we really are as sacred, spiritual beings. As we enter this new millennium of higher consciousness, more and more people are waking up to their true divine natures. As I explain in my book *Born to Be Blessed*, we are, each one of us, blessed by our loving Creator from birth with power, love, creativity, eternal life, perfection, divinity, and a holy interconnectedness with all of creation.

A lot of human violence is out there for all to see on the news every day. Violence to animals, on the other hand, is mostly hidden from view in slaughterhouses, experimental laboratories, puppy mills, zoos, circuses, Premarin horse farms, dairies, factory farms, and many other places where billions of animals and their children suffer and die every day at the hands of human beings.

So we see the human violence and we want it to end, and that is very much in our hearts as people of compassion. I believe we can bring it to an end, but not without ending the war waged by humans against animals. The two stagger along hand in hand waiting for the same miracle that the Universe longs for. They are waiting for us to *wake up our love.*

If we work for an end to human violence and ignore the animals by continuing to contribute to their hidden suffering, we are chasing our tails. We cannot end human suffering alone. It is not a separate entity. Many books have been written that eloquently prove this intricate connection.

For example, in *Sacred Cows and Golden Geese* Drs. Ray and Jean Swingle Greek give us one case after another of animal experiments which have led to human disease or death for the simple reason that animal bodies are so biologically different from human bodies that results from non-human species cannot be extrapolated to our species. Thus, billions of animals throughout human history have suffered and died, and human beings have gained virtually no value from the experiments. Instead, human suffering has been the result of these misguided experiments, because many drugs that were safe for animals caused disease and death to human beings. This is a classic example of a simple truth. Violence can never heal. It only produces more violence.

The Golden Rule of doing unto others as we would have them do to us, also known as the Law of Cause and Effect, is universally taught. If we cause pain in the world, we will reap pain. If we sow love, we will harvest love.

Love Heals Fear

Cruelty to animals is a symptom of global human fear. This fear derives from our early evolutionary origins as a species that had to fight for survival under harsh conditions. As hunter-gatherers, we were fearful, which helped us avoid danger and stay alive. But today, the same fear of loss of power, food, and life is causing global destruction. Mega-corporations, governments, and we consumers are bringing the earth to the brink of destruction. Long ago the victims of fear were tribes and animals who invaded the wrong territory at the wrong time. In recent history and today the victims are entire species, entire cultures and peoples, forests, rivers, and seas.

We are all participating in this fear-driven destruction to some degree through our support of this behavior. The universal human desires for power, freedom, safety, and a full stomach, coupled with the fear of losing those same things, has so far prevented us from stopping the suffering and the destruction.

All the wounds of earth life have been caused by fear. But there is hope! Love can heal those wounds, because love conquers fear. And Love is as available to us as air. We residents of planet earth are embarking together on a massive elevation of consciousness to a higher level than we have ever before attained. It is happening now, all around us and within us. It is time for big dreams and miracles.

In a well-known novel (which I shall not name lest I ruin the ending for you) an evil being holds a small town hostage. He seems to be invincible and begins killing members of the town one by one. With each murder he leaves behind the puzzling message that he will leave if only they will give him what he wants. Of course, as we near the end of the book, we are on the edge of our seats wondering what he wants. Finally, he holds a town meeting and tells the people what they must do in order to get rid of him: they must give him one of their children, or he will kill them all. He wants the child to be his own apprentice, destined for a life filled with evil.

The majority votes to sacrifice one of the children to save themselves, seeing no alternative. The evil being keeps his promise, leaves with the child, and the townspeople remain alive but utterly without wisdom or hope, for they have given up a part of themselves.

This is where we are today. There is fear energy on earth (within us) promising us our lives if we will only sacrifice our innocents to it and look the other way. This is a major crossroad for us. We are at the town meeting, and it's time to vote. Are we going to stand together fearlessly and hold our faith in the power of Love and in our own integrity and bring the Divine plan of Heaven to Earth?

Or are we going to continue to be intimidated by the inner and outer forces that claim to have power over us? When we reclaim our power, we reclaim our divinity, and when we reclaim our divinity, we become the new Compassionate Human, and then *there shall be no war anymore*.

Do you believe in us? in the power of our collective thoughts for good? in our Higher Power's unfailing assistance? in the universal prophecies that heaven can come to earth? that we can choose to create more Love on earth than has ever before been experienced? If you do or if you want to be convinced, please, read on.

Affirmative Prayer Power

Inner peace, whether it is for an individual or for the entire planet, takes place when we remember that Divine Perfection is everywhere present. If we see illness, violence, or degradation, it is because we are looking at the outer appearance. It is possible, as mystics and shamans have demonstrated, to be wholly conscious of the presence of the Holy Oneness in all things. It is by focusing on that presence that great saints through the ages have seen through the veil or *maya* or illusion of "evil" and brought "miraculous" healings that already existed out into visibility.

Metaphysical systems utilize the concept of affirmative prayer. The basis of such prayer is that negative appearances of disease and fear have no power. Only Truth, which is Love, has real, lasting power. By affirming the Truth we align ourselves with the universe and add energy to the relentless movement toward bringing Love everywhere into visibility. The Creator, the Universe, All-That-Is never ceases to fill our cups with Love whether we see it happening or not.

Paradise Found

Animal advocacy is an issue of great importance. No longer can it be discredited as a flaky, fringe fantasy.

Animal rights is a global challenge that has deep spiritual significance for every woman, man, and child on the planet and for every being on the planet.

What do we spell when we put People and Animal Rights together with Ahimsa (Gandhi's vow of nonviolence), Divine Intent, and a Sustainable Environment?

PARADISE
Exactly!

A bit corny, perhaps, but it's my way of putting into **bold** relief the reality that compassion for animals is a puzzle piece that cannot be left out. In our quest for peace on earth, for an earthly paradise, and for inner spiritual joy, we must build a Cosmic Ark and leave no one behind.

> *They will neither harm nor destroy on all my holy mountain for the earth will be full of the knowledge of the Lord.*—Isaiah 11:9

Author's Note
When even the stones are found holy,
no war will be fought, nor hunger found.

I wrote this book *to help us focus our spirits, minds, and hearts* on the liberation of animals, and *to help us focus our spirits, minds, and hearts* on the global shift in consciousness

- from Harm to Harmony,
- from Cruelty to Compassion,
- and from widespread violence to world peace.

This is a spiritually oriented book in the sense that it engages our spirit. It asks for a holistic approach to animal liberation—not just the use of our bodies and minds but our spirits as well.

If you have a strong bias against religion, spirituality, certain types of religion, or a belief in the unseen, please hear me out. I was an atheist from 1964 to 1979, partly because of Christianity's apparent lack of concern for animals and the earth. Worshipping God as a teenager in an Episcopal church full of weekend hunters and fur-wrapped matrons made no sense to me.

But in 1979, a whale and a Native American medicine man known as Mad Bear opened my heart to an entirely new way of looking at and being with God, the Great Spirit. From Mad Bear I learned that the emptiness I felt in the church of my youth was a result of its disconnection from the physical body and lack of reverence for nature and non-human life. The Native American religion, along with many other belief systems, understands that the Divine Creative Energy dwells in all of Creation and that what we do to any part of it we do to ourselves, because we are all one. As Gandhi said, "God is even in these stones."

My philosophical and religious views may differ widely from many of yours, but we do hold a common vision. We all have hope that all animals will someday be treated with the same respect that we give to each other. We all have hope that someday we will live together in peace, all humans and all animals.

Religion aside, scientific studies are showing with increasing frequency that a commonly held vision or thought form, if held long enough and with enough belief in its truth, will eventually break out of the realm of thought and into physical manifestation.

The animals need us all. There is no power greater than LOVE. The prayer tower at Silent Unity in Unity Village, Missouri, has a saying, "What one heart cannot bear alone, a hundred loving hearts can bear with faith." Thank you for loving.

In my meditations, I have felt energy and wisdom coming to me from many animals, as well as from St. Francis, Jesus, Albert Schweitzer, Gandhi, and others who are dedicated to Love and Light and Peace. In many ways, this book is from them as well as from me. Thank You, God, for making us all part of this Divine, Loving Universe.

Every thought is a prayer.
Therefore, let us
Think compassion
Think love
Think peace
For all beings everywhere.
Every act is a prayer.
Therefore, let us
Be compassion
Be love
Be peace
For all beings everywhere.

PART ONE

THE VISION
*A New Millennium of
Compassion for All Beings*

Chapter One

REVERENCE FOR ALL LIFE
A Path to World Peace and Inner Peace

Songs around the Campfire

It was a lively group of folks, an interesting bunch, having dedicated their lives on earth to such huge issues as peace, consciousness raising, and reverence for life. It seems John Denver had just recently arrived and was sitting by a pleasant campfire singing a song they all loved. It was "I Want to Live"—you know, the one about the humpback whales, the children, and the dolphins all singing together asking for the killing and the hunger to stop. When he finished that one, everyone honored the reverent moment with clasped hands and bowed heads.

The evening air was crisp and cool. Smoke from the crackling fire rose straight up—a white plume drifting skyward. Gandhi sat gazing at the orange and yellow flames. He was trying to think of the name of one of his favorite songs that he had heard John sing—something about taking food right out of the mouths of the babies. "Ah," he remembered, "John, can you sing 'What Are We Making Weapons For?' It's one of my favorites." Just then St. Francis remembered his favorite. "John, after that will you sing the one about how can the battle be over if animals are still running from the sound of guns?" "You mean 'And You Say That the Battle is Over,' " said John, "one of my favorites, too. Sure, I'll sing both of those." And John began to sing. Some joined in and sang along, their voices filled with emotion. Some choked back tears.

When the songs were finished, John leaned his guitar against a nearby tree. He looked around at the gathering of peacemakers: Jesus was there, and so were Buddha, St. Francis, Gandhi, Albert Schweitzer, Mother Teresa, Thomas Edison, Albert Einstein, and Rachel Carson. The topic for the evening, as usual, was "How on earth are we going to create world peace?" Like John, they all saw the essential connection between kindness to animals and world peace. Mother Teresa was the first to speak. After thanking John for his heartfelt music, she exclaimed, "*A person who shows cruelty to these creatures cannot be kind to other humans.* Until human beings are instruments of peace to all beings, there will be no peace on earth."[1] Gandhi nodded in agreement. He said that the way a country treats the animals who live there tells one clearly the level of that country's *greatness and moral progress*. "All countries are currently engaged in abysmal practices regarding animals. Many of the people of India are more cruel to animals now than when I was living on earth," he said sadly.

Thomas Edison said, "People need to realize that *nonviolence leads to the highest ethics, which is the goal of all evolution. Until [humans] stop harming all other living beings, [they] are still savage.*"[2] Einstein and Schweitzer spoke of their frequent efforts while they were on earth to get people to widen their circle of compassion and to create a boundless ethic that included all life. Einstein talked about the many human beings who don't understand that they are part of the whole universe, not separate from other beings, but connected. "It is this delusion that humans are separate that keeps us imprisoned," he said. "*[Their] task must be to free [them]selves by widening [their] circle of compassion to embrace all living creatures and the whole of nature in its beauty.*" Schweitzer agreed, saying, "Yes, that's absolutely correct. *Until man extends his circle of compassion to include all living things, man will not himself find peace.*" That's the way it is, they agreed—no way around it.

Rachel Carson nodded slowly and sighed. "Yes, I agree with everyone. *We cannot have peace among men, whose hearts delight in killing any living creature. By*

*every act that glorifies or even tolerates such moronic
delight in killing we set back the progress of humanity."*
As they talked on into the evening it became clear that
the unanimous conclusion was that, as long as people
wear fur coats and eat meat or abuse animals in any
way, there will be wars on earth.

Jesus gazed lovingly at the group. He asked everyone to consider how they could help humanity understand that the instruction to love one another meant to
love all beings, not just human ones. Buddha added,
"Yes, the human dream of world peace will simply not
come true until that wisdom becomes a part of the global consciousness."

St. Francis offered some comforting thoughts. He
said "I have been called the patron saint of ecology, of
peace, and of animals. That shows us that people see, at
the spirit level, that these three ideals are connected.
Deep down, I believe people understand that ecology,
peace, and reverence for life cannot exist without each
other. There will be no inner peace or world peace for
humans without peace for animals, and there will be no
healing of the earth and humans without a healing of
the animal nations." Francis continued, "We have all
taught them with our lives and our words. John has
taught them with his music. Many other teachers have
taught this as well, and many more are now on earth
sharing this great truth, more than there ever have been.
I feel very hopeful, but I think we need to send lots of

love and support to these teachers and to all the people and beings of earth. Let us hold them in our hearts lovingly and visualize the earth as the heaven she can most certainly become." Everyone nodded to each other in silent and reverent agreement, and John began to sing.

> *Finding peace within and bringing peace to the world may start with the capacity to look into another's eyes and recognize there a kindred soul, whether the eyes belong to a German, a Dutchman, a friend, a chimpanzee, or a wolf.*
> —Gary Kowalski[3]

While Visions of Peace Dance in Our Heads
We must turn back to what we have left of the capacity for wonder; only reverence for life can deliver us from our inhumanity, and from the cataclysm of violence awaiting us at the end of our present road.—Laurens van der Post[4]

Most people want to live in a peaceful, compassionate world in which there are no wars and all people have enough to eat, a chance to learn and follow their dreams, and a safe place to live and love. But as long as the animals and the earth continue to suffer, peace on earth eludes us. As long as our relations in the animal and other nations are experiencing violence at our hands, human wars and misery will continue, because we are connected to all life. The suffering of one is the suffering of all, just as the joy and peace of one is the joy and peace of all. We cannot disconnect ourselves from the intimate, intricate circle of life.

We human beings are in the process of creating a holistic vision that includes, as St. Francis and the others so dramatically exemplified in their lives, peace for people, peace for animals, and peace for the earth. In this holy vision, let us imagine a world in which all people are free and empowered, and all the animals are free as well. Imagine them free to be who they are, to do their favorite things, and to live with their families in the jungles and forests and plains. Imagine their homes being respected, the forests left free to grow, the waters flowing clean and pure again. Imagine the pharmaceutical and soap companies, fur businesses, corporate giants, ranchers, factory farm corporations, and crews of giant fishing fleets transforming their companies to operate from an ethic of harmlessness and compassion. Perhaps some of these companies' decision makers begin to see the light and realize that all life is sacred, while others transform their business practices because fewer and fewer people will buy their products as long as they are harming animals.

Imagine scientists all over the world searching for good homes for the millions of chimpanzees and other primates, beagles, rabbits, rats, and all the others who have spent their lives in confinement, loneliness, and pain in medical and scientific laboratories. All over the world, hunters and trappers bury their guns and traps in symbolic gestures of solidarity with the animals. Meanwhile, the animals themselves begin destroying traps and begin communicating telepathically with hunters that they simply want to live.

Sound fantastic? Impossible? Liz Williamson, a primatologist studying gorillas in war-torn Rwanda, has observed that the gorillas are learning new behaviors in response to the war. In particular, the gorillas have begun destroying the deadly snare traps that have been set in the jungles.[5]

Let us envision the slaughterhouses shutting down, one by one, for lack of demand for meat and because they cannot find enough people willing to kill all day long anymore. Fences begin disintegrating, and many farm animals begin to adapt to living free and keeping their families together. Some choose to stay and help their human companions, and others find homes in the hundreds of animal sanctuaries that already exist today.

Just imagine!

To create such a world would require millions of hearts to join in a symphony of compassion and hold this beautiful vision of true peace on earth *for all beings.* When violence to animals ceases, then violence to humans will cease, because we will finally be living our true nature. It is a fantastic dream, but let us dare to dream it.

*The wolf will live with the lamb, the leopard
will lie down with the goat, the calf and the lion
and the yearling together; and a little child will
lead them. The cow will feed with the bear,
their young will lie down together, and the lion
will eat straw like the ox. The infant will play
near the hole of the cobra, and the young child
put his hand into the viper's nest. They will neither harm nor destroy on all my holy mountain, for the earth will be full of the knowledge
of the Lord as the waters cover the sea.*
                                    —Isaiah 11:6–9

We are all peacemakers. We are endowed with the
power of thought and the power of prayer. What we
think about expands. What we give our attention to is
attracted to us. We have the power to multiply love
vibrations exponentially. By focusing our hearts and
minds and actions on love, we can co-create with the
Creative Force of the Universe a world at peace for all
beings. We are maturing as a species. We are growing in
consciousness to a new level of spiritual awareness.
What an exciting time to be living on earth!

The Science of Vision Holding
We cannot allow ourselves to be overwhelmed and dis-
couraged by the voices of negative thinkers and cynics
who believe we cannot manifest this dream. We must
not allow our hearts to contract.

The importance of carrying this vision goes way beyond wishful thinking. It is scientific. The field theory of reality in quantum physics suggests that the real substance of the universe is not the solid matter that we see. That solid matter that we think we see is actually 99% empty space. That includes our own bodies. The real substance is found in the fields of energy—electromagnetic, gravitational, and quantum fields. What is important to us here is that physicists tell us that whatever happens in one part of the field affects the whole.

Each of us, and the universe too, are fields of energy, and we are all affecting each other's energy fields. Every thought, every word, and every act of violence, whether to people or animals or the earth, affects the entire cosmic energy field.

The "observer effect" demonstrated by quantum physicists teaches us that the intention of an observer of quantum phenomena directly affects the results of quantum experiments. There is some sort of cosmic communication that goes on, though we are largely unaware of it, between our thoughts and the energy fields of the universe. Gordon Davidson, cofounder of the Center for Visionary Leadership, suggests that we may cause more violence to occur simply by observing it, such as in the news and movies. He asks, "Could the constant observation of thousands of acts of violence by a large segment of earth's population be, in fact, causing more of it to be perpetrated on all of us?"[6]

This certainly fits with the ageless wisdom that energy follows thought, and that as you think, so you are. The power of the imagination to create is staggering. With the help of science and spiritual teachings, we are grasping this truth better every day. My friend A.J. sits with her grandchildren before bedtime, when she can, and together they look at books full of pictures of beautiful things. The purpose?—so their dreams will be filled with beauty.

Perhaps the most important thing we can do is to realize fully that each one of our thoughts is sending out either destructive or creative energy to the world and to life. Our collective thoughts, focused firmly on peace, tossing seeds of peace up into the winds of grace, can and will bring heaven home.

Humanity's Dark Night of the Soul: This May Be Our Biggest Test

Out of compost comes a blossom;
Out of manure comes a vine;
From the fallen tree, a mushroom;
From the scorched prairie, grass.
So the bison follows the flames
and finds a feast.

Anyone who has lived more than a few years has experienced the hero's journey, sometimes known as the dark night of the soul. Mythologically or symbolically speaking, the hero's journey begins when the hero in the story leaves his or her familiar home and goes off in search of a great prize of one sort or another. After a multitude of encounters with dragons, witches, and various other dreaded "enemies," the hero finally succeeds and returns home to share the wisdom or riches gained.

We repeat this story many times in our lives, as we face one challenge after another. The key to being victorious in these stories is that the hero must come to understand that she or he is not a victim and that the dragons and witches are not enemies but teachers. Beauty discovered that Beast was not a monster after all but a handsome prince. Once love was given freely, the true nature of the beast was revealed and united with Beauty. In that way they both became healed and whole. This is the story of all our own inner healings. It is also the story of the healing of the world.

We are here in temporary bodies trying to get the physical realm in sync with the spiritual realm. The spiritual realm is perfect. As in the spiritual realm, so be it in the physical realm. The monster of human violence and war is our teacher. Its lesson is that *it* is an illusion. Like the beast and the dragons and witches, it will continue to roar and breathe fire and cast spells on us until we wake up and realize that it has no real power, no real existence. The only real power is in the Divine Energy of Love, also known as God or the Higher Power that lives within each of us.

It is as if God is the source of light for a great movie projector. We provide the film of our lives, and the picture is then projected on the screen. God's light is the pure truth, but the film we create can distort the Creator's light. The more distorted our view of life and the more powerless and victimized we feel, the more unpleasant our movie will seem to be. But the truth is always there in the light Itself. Just as Beauty's beast transfigured into a handsome prince when she truly loved him, our lives are transfigured when we let go of our attachments to what we think we see and love the essence of life itself longing to live.

In all the hero tales, the hero is challenged to face what is most terrifying, embrace the opportunity, and not shrink back in fear. Each challenge is a chance to let go of fear. Gandhi walks up to the dragon and says, "This is wrong, and I won't sit down or shut up until it is made right."

A Zen proverb says, "Everything you meet along the path is yourself." The challenges of war, human violence, and animal suffering are all us; all reflections of what goes on inside each of us. All of it asks us to see beyond the appearance of ugliness and beyond the taut tension between good and evil. "Jump," it says. "Jump up higher—see the beauty hidden within the ugliness." As Ram Dass said, "[E]ach situation is being presented by your Guru to bring you home."[7]

On a personal level, in our own lives, we usually sense when it is time to embark on our next journey.

Things have been warm and safe for a while, and then the insistent longing of soul begins—a sort of scary and seductive magnetic pull that draws us away from that safety and points us toward mysterious, untraveled roads. We know we must follow this fearful bliss or we will stagnate and die. There's pain ahead. We know that. But the reward is so great, we must go clambering after it against all odds.

As with us, so goes the collective consciousness as well. As a species, we are embarking on a most remarkable hero's journey. The prize is no small pot of gold. The prize is world peace for everyone. On the spirit level, this peace already exists waiting for us to be able to see it behind the veil of violence we have created. Chaos, war, animal cruelty, greed, and arrogance will continue to cast their images on the movie screen of our collective world until enough of us take our places next to the Great Projectionist and replace that old worn-out film with our new story—and watch the bison ambling over for some of that fresh, green grass.

The Animal Cruelty–Human Violence Connection

Since 1945, roughly 25 million people have been killed in over 100 conflicts. Of those 25 million people, 95 percent of those were innocent men, women, and children.[8] In addition to the people lost, billions of innocent animals were killed. Add this to the unknown numbers of violent deaths and the suffering of billions more people and animals due to greed and quests for power in the entertainment, corporate, scientific, and medical industries.

Recent studies report that many serial killers, criminals, and corrupt dictators had histories of torturing animals before they moved on to human violence. Serial killers such as Jeffrey Dahmer and Ted Bundy abused and killed animals without remorse.[9] In a study of several recent school shootings, many of the children involved had abused animals. For example, Andrew Golden, who, with Mitchell Johnson, killed four students and a teacher in Jonesboro, Arkansas, was known as a boy who "shoots dogs all the time with a .22."[10] The FBI actually uses reports of animal cruelty to help them predict the potential violence of suspected and known criminals. Research has proven that animal abusers commit up to five times as many crimes as non-animal abusers.[11] Margaret Mead said: "One of the most dangerous things that can happen to a child is to kill or torture an animal and get away with it."[12]

Some years ago when I lived in a small town in Missouri, I heard that the Dairy Council was "loaning" rats to grade schools along with lesson plans for the teachers. Innocently, the teachers were proceeding with the "experiments" to teach good nutrition to their students. The experiments went like this: Each classroom was given two rats in separate cages. The children were to feed one rat "junk food" which consisted of Coke (no water), French fries, and other unwholesome foods. The other rat was fed a supposedly "healthy" diet. The children then watched as the first rat suffered alone and grew weaker by the day. Following the experiment, the Dairy Council promised to pick up the rats and "dispose of" them.

After hearing about this plan, I contacted the school principals and asked them to consider with me what the real lesson was in this experiment. First of all, it teaches nothing about human nutrition, since rats and humans are different physiologically. More importantly, it conveys the very clear message that we as human beings have the right to incarcerate, separate, abuse, and finally kill helpless creatures. In fact, the program teaches that we not only have the right to do those things, but that we must do them in order to get good grades, please the teacher, and be accepted by the group. It desensitizes children to violence done to helpless creatures in a most subtle and harmful way.

Thankfully, the principals to whom I spoke agreed with me and declined the Dairy Council's offer. That may seem like a very small victory, and it is on the physical plane. But on the spiritual plane, I believe that many rats felt the impact of the effort that was made on behalf of their nation. Every time one of us or a group of us moves toward the animal nations in peace and with the intent to honor, help, or learn from them, we are changing the very vibratory fabric of the universe.

We cannot create peace on earth for humans unless we create peace on earth for all our relations. And we cannot create external peace unless we develop internal peace. The three—peace for animals and the earth, peace for people, and inner, spiritual peace—cannot exist without each other. Separately, the existence of each is only a fragment of a dream. Together, they are the healing of the world.

We have viewed the earth as predators long enough. Indeed, we have become cannibals, because we eat our own kin. Our predatory nature derives from fear of loss, starvation, and death. Fear leads to violence among human beings and adds fear vibrations to the planet. Every time a poacher kills another gorilla or a slaughterhouse employee numbs himself to the violence he engages in all day, fear vibrations resonate far and wide and affect us all, because we are all so intimately interconnected.

For centuries we human beings have justified slavery and war by convincing ourselves that the slaves and the enemies were inferior or weren't "human." R.R. Cobb, a proponent of slavery in the mid-1800s, said, "A state of bondage, so far from doing violence to the laws of nature, develops and perfects it; in that state (the Negro) enjoys the greatest amount of happiness and arrives at the greatest degree of perfection, of which his nature is capable."[13] The same has been said of women, who for so long were considered "chattel" or property (and still are in some countries). The same has been said of the native peoples of every country on earth, and of all peoples who have been attacked, enslaved, and otherwise treated as the "inferior other." And the same has been said of all the animals of earth. It is this idea of separation and difference that has justified the most outrageous perpetrations of human and animal cruelty. And it is this idea of separation and difference that has caused our desperate loneliness and restlessness of spirit.

Why do human beings seem so intent on fixing a distance between themselves and the other animals? Why has it been so important to limit them to the status of unfeeling possessions? Could it be we fear our own interior animal nature? Could it be that we keep them in cages or send them running from our guns and knives because we are terrified of the wild within us? If we let loose our own wild selves, would we become werewolves or vampires? Our favorite monster movies are clear indications of our fears of the wild within us and the need to destroy it.

Clarissa Pinkola Estes, author and Jungian analyst, says, "We are all filled with a longing for the wild," and yet society teaches us to feel shame for such yearning. But, shamed or not, "the shadow of the wild woman still lurks behind us during our days and in our nights. No matter where we are, the shadow that trots behind us is definitely four-footed."[14]

Author and animal advocate Bill Schul has discussed this matter at length with Native Americans who have maintained their comfortable intimacy with the animal nations. "The Indian tells us," says Schul, "that if we wish to dance with wolves, rather than experiencing them as life separate from ourselves, we first find them within ourselves. Then the dance can begin."[15]

Animal Ambassadors of Peace

One day a woman was walking along the shore of the Payaswami River in India holding her baby. As she walked, somehow her baby slipped out of her arms and fell into the river. The mother screamed in terror. She didn't know how to swim. She was paralyzed with fear. Just then, a monkey sitting in a tree nearby leaped into the swiftly flowing river and swam to the baby. The mother watched fearfully, not knowing what would happen next. Then, to her amazement, the little monkey brought the baby back to shore and laid the infant at the woman's feet.[16] This brings to mind Carl Sagan's penetrating question, "How smart does a chimp have to be before killing him constitutes murder?"[17]

Meanwhile, as you read this, each year in the U.S. over 60,000 primates, very much like this little monkey hero, are being tortured and killed in the name of science with toxic chemicals, electric shock, surgical procedures, and deprivation. Many times the monkeys have been observed doing whatever they can to reduce the suffering of other monkeys. Rhesus monkeys, for example, will not pull levers that bring them food if pulling the lever will deliver a shock to another monkey. They choose to go hungry rather than cause pain to a friend.[18] Certainly they would agree with the Reverend V.A. Holmes-Gore, an Anglican priest, when he said, "We cannot hope to rid the world of war, disease, and a hundred other evils until we learn to show compassion to other creatures and refrain from taking their lives for food, clothing, or pleasure."[19]

Old Smoke, a horse who lived at the Guadalupe Ranch in Arizona, was usually very polite and easygoing. But one day, he began bucking and rearing in his corral until he broke through a section and ran off. The ranch hands jumped on their horse companions and followed in hot pursuit, amazed at Old Smoke's uncharacteristic behavior. They chased him for seven miles out onto the hot desert. Finally he stopped. To the great shock of the ranch hands, Old Smoke had led them straight to his friend Kelvin Jones, who lay injured on the desert sand. This great horse hero somehow intuitively realized his friend was in trouble and knew exactly where to find him, and he risked harm to himself in order to save him.[20] Meanwhile, over 75,000 pregnant horses are being kept confined in tiny stalls in Canada and the United States. For six months of every year, they are unable to exercise or turn around, are forced to stand in their own waste, and are deprived of adequate water, affection, and veterinary attention. Their babies are taken from them at one or two months, and most of the foals are slaughtered for human and animal consumption. Then the mothers are reimpregnated and forced to stand in the stalls again year after year until they no longer produce adequately the urine that is collected from them. This urine is collected to make the estrogen replacement drugs known as Premarin, Prempro, Prempac, and Premphase.[21] (For more information, please go to my Web site at www.premarin-free.com.)

Monty Roberts, the famous "horse whisperer," demonstrates his remarkable ability to communicate with horses in such a way that they want to be with him and cooperate with his gentle training methods. He often demonstrates his method to groups of people by going into a ring with a horse that has been abused. Usually in less than an hour, he gains the horse's trust, and she allows him to get on her back. Monty has noted that very often, at the moment when the horse begins to show that she trusts him, several people in the audience will faint or have strong emotional reactions. In questioning them, he has found that all these people have been physically abused themselves and had unconsciously identified with the abused horse. We are indeed intimately connected to all life. Anytime one being is healed, we all gain something beautiful from that healing.[22]

Finding Inner Peace through the Power
of Reverence for Life

*Those whose minds are at peace and who are
free from passions do not desire to live at the
expense of others.*—Lacharanga Sutra

Only when we recognize our oneness with all life do
we find the inner peace for which we long. I believe we
are learning that every person on earth is a spiritual
brother or sister. I believe we are beginning to expand
the circle of compassion beyond our species, as that
monkey did on the Payaswami River, to include all
beings, all species, all life. Just as the monkey and Old
Smoke crossed species boundaries to save a baby and a
man, we are also crossing these boundaries to save the
monkeys and the horses.

The simplest way I know of to explain what sort of
new creature we are becoming is this: we are feeling less
fear and more love and inner peace. That inner peace
leads to and comes from reverence for life. And that reverence for life leads to peace on earth.

*It is my greatest hope that our movement [ani-
mal rights], which has often been maligned as
unimportant by advocates of other causes, will
ultimately be recognized for its unique and
invaluable contribution to people's ability to
live peacefully among each other. The end of*

violence to animals and the end of violence to human beings must, in the final analysis, occur together as one event.—Elliot M. Katz, D.V.M., President, In Defense of Animals

When you and I experience transcendent love, even if it is only for a moment, that single feeling literally transforms the world a little bit more. As peacemakers, all of us are on a mission to teach love and to heal fear. We are bringing in a new century of compassion. The Buddha said, "All beings tremble before violence. All fear death. All love life. See yourself in others. Then whom can you hurt? What harm can you do?"

Do we truly want world peace and inner peace? If we do then we must stop wearing and eating our relatives. We must give up torturing and enslaving our brothers and sisters.

Do we want inner peace and world peace? I can imagine St. Francis, at this point, dropping by to see us after his evening with John Denver and the others. He might answer something like this—"We all want the peace you are talking about, but if you have men who will exclude any of God's creatures from the shelter of compassion and pity, you will have men who will deal likewise with their fellow men. And furthermore," he would say, "not to hurt our humble brethren is our first duty to them, but to stop there is not enough. We have a higher mission—to be of service to them wherever they require it." Yes, we want inner peace and world peace, but to get it we must open our arms in a much wider embrace. We can't have our peace and eat it too.

It is here in the heart of harmlessness to all, here in the boundless circle of compassion, here in the giving of service to the voiceless and the helpless—it is here we find our true and lasting joy. It is here that heaven finally finds itself here with us on earth.

> *Only spiritual consciousness—realization of God's presence in oneself and in every other living being—can save the world. I see no chance for peace without it. Begin with yourself. There is no time to waste. It is your duty to do your part to bring God's kingdom on earth.*
>
> —Paramahansa Yogananda[24]

Chapter Two

THE AWAKENING OF HUMANITY TO COMPASSION

Let us become the change we seek in the world.
—Gandhi

We Are Living in Phenomenal Times:

- Willis Harman, founder of the Institute of Noetic Sciences, calls this the time of the "Global Mind Change."[1]
- James Twyman, the "peace troubadour," declares this to be the time of "The Great Awakening."[2]
- Gregg Braden, scientist and author, notes that all religions have predicted this "Shift of the Ages" or "Christing of Earth."[3]
- Jean Houston, co-director of the Foundation for Mind Research, author, scholar, and philosopher, calls it "Jump Time" and us the "Possible Humans."[4]
- Barbara Marx Hubbard, founder of the Center for Conscious Evolution, calls this the time of the birth of the Universal Human.[5]
- Matthew Fox, author and director of the Institute of Culture and Creation Spirituality, calls this time the "Global Renaissance" heralded by the "coming of the Cosmic Christ."[6]
- This time is also known as the Age of Aquarius, the Coming of the Great Paradigm Shift, the Emergence of the Divine Feminine, the Global Initiation into Compassion and Wholeness, the end of victim consciousness, and the advent of personal empowerment.

Humankind is about to wake up and become Kindhuman, the Humane Being that creation has long been anticipating. Harm is transforming into harmony. "Evilution" is turning into evolution for the good of all. We are, as Pierre Teilhard de Chardin declared, "a new humanity coming into form." The energy is rising. We're about to sing the next note in our uni-verse, a love song of connectedness with all creation. We're journeying along a new road guided by the compass of compassion.

Becoming *Homo Ahimsa*

I'm going to add one more name to the list that describes the glorious human beings we are becoming. My name for the new human is *Homo ahimsa*. Ahimsa is the Sanskrit word for harmlessness, compassion, and unconditional love for all beings. In Chapter Four, I describe ahimsa in more detail.

As we evolve to a higher level of consciousness, that consciousness will bring with it a burning desire to transform the ways we live in relation to animals. Killing and harming animals will simply not be an option to *Homo ahimsa*.

We are at the precipice of a spiritual challenge of extraordinary proportions. There is cosmic energy rising around us. We are immersed in it. Heaven and Earth are handing out invitations right and left to embark on this spectacular voyage into a future of peace and compassion.

But we could still fail. This spiritual challenge is not being forced upon us. We can choose to live in love, or we can choose to live in fear. As Gary Zukav explains in his book *Seat of the Soul*, we can choose to remain locked in our five senses and pursue external power as we have done for centuries, or we can develop into a species that lives from authentic, inner, spiritual power.[7]

Since the beginning of creation, everything in the universe has been moving steadily forward, glacier-like, into increasing perfection and awareness. Our spirits and the spirits of all beings are our god selves, invisible to most of us, eternal in nature, absolutely tuned to Divine Harmony, Peace, Compassion, and Reverence for Life. They always have been and always will be. But our technology has raced ahead of our ethics. We're playing "catch-up" now, catching up with the wisdom of our spirits, our true nature.

> *The yearning for our lost perfection, the urge to do and be that which is the noblest, the most beautiful of which we are capable, is the creative impulse of every high achievement. We strive for perfection here because we long to be restored to our oneness with God.*
>
> —Paramahansa Yogananda[8]

Gandhi called himself an optimist on the subject of our evolving toward the good because of his "unflinch-

ing faith that right must prosper in the end.""⁹ Whenever
we act or think in accord with the inner, divine rhythm
of our own spirits, we experience tremendous joy,
because we are in tune with our god selves. It's kind of
like biofeedback; perhaps we could call it spirit-feed-
back. If we are experiencing cosmic joy, whatever we did
to reach that, we want to do it again.

Because of this innate attraction to perfection that
we all share, all creation has been drawn day and night,
century after century in that direction. Only the deep-
seated fears of our personal identities or egos that mis-
takenly think we are alone and attacked, keep us from
our high flying dreams. But the momentum, the movement toward liberation cannot be stopped. Here we are
at the very beginning of the twenty-first century, and
things are getting very interesting.

Heaven Within Us

Gary Zukav says we are capable of developing a sensory system beyond the five senses. This new sensory system is intuition. Living intuitively has been a path for a
rare few saints, shamans, mystics, and others until
recently. However, now it seems that living beyond the
five senses is becoming a reality for multitudes.

As a species, limited to our five senses, we have
throughout history tried to control the physical world. It
is this fearful effort that has led to so much violence and
destruction. Now, as we make this evolutionary leap, we

are understanding that we are not here to control the external world at all. No! We are here to harmonize our internal worlds and in that manner find true joy. What a leap!

Imagine the results of that kind of consciousness on planet earth. That is what is meant by finding the Kingdom of Heaven within. That is what is meant by bringing Heaven to Earth. That is what Christians pray for when they pray "Thy will be done, in earth as it is in Heaven." Imagine the results—peace within each one of us; peace among nations; peace among species. That's the leap we are being asked to take. Will we take it? It's our choice. I believe we will.

You and I want to see compassion reign on earth. We want animal suffering to end; indeed, we want all suffering to end. I am saying that it can happen, but not without our focused intent.

Many of us have long been caught up in the same mindset as the economic and political powers whose policies perpetuate suffering. It is the mindset that *we* are right and *they* are wrong, and somehow *we* have to change *them*. We are learning. We are learning that no one can change someone else. We can only change ourselves. We're also learning that we are one united family. We all come from the same Divine Parent Creator. We all are equally adored and valuable. We all are moving inexorably, with God's help, in the direction of perfected compassion and love.

What this means is that as we work on ourselves, bringing ourselves into more joy and peace, we affect (not control) everyone else because of our sacred interconnectedness. And this is the great beacon of light that shines ahead for us, beckoning us on. There is hope, and it is here shining more brightly in this time than perhaps ever before. We have a chance to grab hold of the hands of the angels who are here working overtime to help us.

All Heaven is in concert with us. We look around and see violence and suffering everywhere in the physical world. It is widely said that our species could self-destruct if we continue to live in fear. But with the evolutionary energy rising now, if enough of us CHOOSE LOVE, we're going to make it.

The old order is breaking down; systems are disintegrating or in extreme transition; chaos fills the news. These are radical times. We are witnessing an extraordinary acceleration of the evolution of consciousness. Disintegration is necessary for reintegration to take place. Order swirls out of chaos. The cosmic, global yearning for peace and kindness is unmistakable. We are dancing, singing, and weaving our way intuitively into this new and much more lovely chapter of earth's story.

It is all a spiral of becoming. The people of your time, toward the end of this century, will be taking the tiller of the world. But you cannot go directly. You have to go in spirals, touching upon every people, every culture, every kind of consciousness. It is there that the noosphere, the field of mind, will awaken, and WE WILL REBUILD THE EARTH . . . .The present chaos is not the end of the world,but the labor pains of a new earth, and a new humanity coming into new form.

—Pierre Teilhard de Chardin[10]

Eisenhower famously said that people want peace much more than their governments and that, in fact, "one of these days governments had better get out of the way and let them have it."

Revelation in the Christian Bible predicts a time when God will "wipe every tear from their eyes. There will be no more death or mourning or crying or pain, for the old order of things has passed away" (Rev. 21: 4).

Will we awaken to who we are and fearlessly allow the Pure Light and Love of the Creator to flow through us to all creation? We can! Will we?

I believe in us. I believe we will. I believe many already have, and the numbers are quickly multiplying. In my book *Born to Be Blessed* I explain who we are at the core of our beings. If you have any doubts within you that you can become an outrageously bountiful fountain of love, please read *Born to Be Blessed*. In it you will find that God has created us all with the same seven blessings. I've reproduced the "Letter from God" from my book here to give you an idea of just how extraordinary we are. We are fully endowed with the power to make the next leap in consciousness that humanity is now poised to make.

A Love Letter to All of Us and All Creation from God
My Beloved Child,

YOU ARE IMMORTAL.

> Your very existence is holy and eternal. Your own divinity is etched upon the universe forever. You will make transitions from this realm to others, but always you will live within Me and I within you as we dance and play together.

YOU BELONG.

> Without you, I would not be complete, nor would Life, nor Love. You are part of the One Divine Cosmic Family. Absolutely everyone and everything is connected in this great sea of Love. Without you We are not whole. You are needed and wanted and adored.

YOU ARE POWERFUL.

> I am the Power of Love. Your cells and your breathing, your thoughts and longings all vibrate with that Power. You breathe in my awesome Love for you and all Creation. You breathe out your electrifying Love for all that is. You are Heaven brought to Earth.

YOU ARE LOVED.

I love you without boundaries or limits. There
is nothing as vast and infinite as My Love for
you. There is nothing you can do that will dis-
suade Me from loving you. You are made of
My Love, and nothing can separate us from
Each Other.

YOU ARE CREATIVE.

Together you and I are Co-Creators. We birth
energy into matter, light into form, Heaven into
Earth, vibration into song. With every child
you comfort, every stroke of your pen, every
word from your lips and every kiss, you can fill
the universe with more beauty, more mystery,
and more Love.

YOU ARE PERFECT.

When you feel lost, alone, different, or full of
faults, remember that you are perfect to Me
right now just as you are. I see only exquisite
beauty and elegance and grace in you, Beloved.
If the world seems to judge you or the path you
have taken, remember there is no "right" path
home to Me. You are already here in My arms
this very day.

YOU ARE DIVINE.

There is nothing in Heaven or Earth that is not
Sacred and filled with Me. I am in all that is, and
all that is lives and breathes in Me. I am Life, and

I am Love. Your spirit sees Me looking back at you from every face, every drop of rain, every stone, every gust of wind. When you look in the mirror, you see your face and mine. There, in you, rejoices the Divine.

Love Forever,

God[11]

Please pause for a moment to breathe,
reflect, receive.

Half Sinners, Half Saints

Because of our blessings, because of our innate goodness, we are capable, as Jane Goodall says, "of the most noble, generous, and heroic behavior." By nature, she points out, we have opposing tendencies, "half sinner, half saint," equally capable of the most despicable violence and the most laudable selflessness.[12]

We have proven beyond all doubt that we can magnify and maximize our propensities for evil. We have brought earth and her innocent children and ourselves to the brink of annihilation. We have quite literally run out of time. The highly esteemed eco-visionary Thomas Berry says, "We must . . . reinvent the human itself." We need "a conversion experience deep in the psychic structure of the human." He calls us to a new global mindset of wonder and intimacy with regard to the natural world. With this paradigm shift in consciousness, instead of the oxymoron of "sustainable development," we will create new ways of living in harmony with each other and with all life.[13]

Albert Einstein famously said, "The most beautiful thing we can experience is the mysterious." What if, prior to the industrial age, human culture had followed the mysterious path mapped out by St. Francis—a path that itself was a holy temple to him? What would the world be like now if *Homo sapiens* had journeyed into the future in intimate kinship with all creation as Francis did? None of the destruction that occurred under the false understanding of "dominion" would have taken place. Would we, then, have the technology we love so much? We would have our vast networks of communication and higher standards of living, no doubt. But, because we would have been operating out of a sense of the sacred, our technology would have been created without harm to other life forms.

A disciple once asked the Buddha, "Would it be true to say that part of our training is for the development of love and compassion?" The Buddha answered, "No, it would not be true to say this. It would be true to say that the whole of our training is for the development of love and compassion." Buddhism teaches that there are three root causes of suffering—greed, hatred, and delusion. This is the world we live in now, full of suffering because of human greed, hatred, and delusion.

The antidotes for these three are generosity, lovingkindness, and wisdom.

The ironically wonderful thing about the fact that we humans have created a world full of suffering is this: We're out of time. The damage is done; the desecration is beyond belief. We have taken free and selfish will to the farthest reaches of imagination. What's so wonderful about that? It's simply that we can't wait anymore. We have to apply the antidotes of generosity, loving kindness, and wisdom now. We can't mess around and think about it and philosophize about it anymore. We must act and act quickly; we must start living and praying as the awakened, loving, sacred, compassionate creatures that we are, and have always been, fully capable of being.

It's a little bit like a first skydiving experience, perhaps. We've talked about it, we've dreamed about it, but now we're up in the plane, and there's somebody behind us ready to give us a shove. No more waiting—we've got to jump now and, as Ray Bradbury has said, build our wings on the way down.

Signs That the New Dawn Is Near

Social scientist Paul Ray has spent the last 13 years working to "identify the population who are predisposed to act to create a new culture, based on both ecological sustainability and spirituality." This is a group, he estimates, of 50 million people whom he calls "cul-

tural creatives." By doing this research he is helping us
to see that we're not alone in our vision for a better
world and that we can accomplish great change by joining together in collective consciousness. He points out
that cultural creatives are found in all social classes,
ethnic groups, and ages. "The only demographic that
stands out is 60 percent women."[14] An interesting sta-
tistic to accompany that one: 80 percent of all members
of humane organizations are women. The Divine
Feminine is alive and well.

Speaking of the Divine Femme, she made a big noise
in Joshua Tree, California on February 21, 2000. It has
long been predicted by Native American prophecy that
when Giant Rock, a huge, sacred rock near Joshua Tree,
split open, that would herald the awakening of the
Divine Feminine in the world and the ushering in of an
era of compassion and peace. On February 21, 2000, a
large portion of this largest freestanding boulder in the
world split off and fell to the ground.[15]

Apologies from high places are signaling a new era
of compassion as well. In March 2000, during the Day
of Pardon Mass at St. Peter's Basilica, Pope John Paul II
asked God to forgive the Roman Catholics for their
atrocities toward Jews, women, and minorities.[16] In
April 2000, the Catholic Church issued a formal apology to Brazil's native peoples for the "sins and errors"
committed by its clergy against the people.[17] These
apologies, while somewhat weak and awfully late, are

nevertheless harbingers of a new humility, a tentative letting go of patriarchal arrogance.

Meanwhile, in September 2000, Kevin Gover, a Pawnee Native American and head of the federal Bureau of Indian Affairs issued a moving apology to Native Americans for the "legacy of racism and inhumanity" perpetrated by the BIA since its inception. "Never again," he declared in his emotional speech, "will we attack your religions, your languages, your rituals, or any of your tribal ways. Never again will we seize your children, nor teach them to be ashamed of who they are. Never again."[18]

On June 26, 2000, 300 people from 39 spiritual traditions and 44 different countries gathered together to sign the historic United Religions Initiative Charter at Carnegie Music Hall in Pittsburgh, Pennsylvania. The Charter begins this way:

United Religions Initiative Charter

We, people of diverse religions, spiritual expressions and indigenous traditions throughout the world, hereby establish the United Religions Initiative to promote enduring, daily interfaith cooperation, to end religiously motivated violence, and to create cultures of peace, justice and healing for the Earth and all living beings.[19]

In September 2000, at the United Nations Millennium Assembly, the Secretary General listed six values that nations need to share: "Freedom; equity and solidarity; tolerance; nonviolence; respect for nature; and shared responsibility."

There is tremendous momentum moving us forward into the reality of peace on earth. There is a great upwelling of spirit going on at this very critical time. Any efforts you make will not be in vain but will add in a mysteriously exponential way to making Love happen.

The Evolution of a New Ethic Toward Animals: From Humanitarians to Omnitarians

Much of what is happening now has been the result of many different groups with different causes working diligently to bring about justice in their own particular area of interest. There are groups focused on liberating political prisoners, eliminating modern slavery, saving whales from slaughter, closing down circuses, ending sweat shop practices, demanding an end to old-growth forest cutting, and liberating animals from experimentation. Some of these come from a spiritual point of view, while others are more secular. There are thousands of groups, both small and large, speaking out for those who cannot speak for themselves. Margaret Mead's well-known words cheer us on: "Never doubt that a small group of thoughtful, committed citizens can change the world; indeed, it is the only thing that ever does."

I believe we are seeing much evidence today of these groups coming together in various ways and seeing that *we have a common vision.* That vision is a world of peace and compassion for all. Although many of these groups are not making mention of animals in their overall plans for peace on earth, they are becoming more open to the idea that there is a connection, that, indeed, we cannot have world peace without peace for animals.

In addition to this next wave of energy coming from these groups for the animals, I also see a new and very large group of people joining us very soon. I am thinking of all the people who have suppressed their sense of mercy for animals for fear of social disapproval and ridicule. They still feel a twinge when they look at the dead bodies on their dinner plates. But social programming is powerful. For centuries the exploitation, torture, and killing of animals has been the accepted norm. We have all been through radical desensitization, encouraged to ignore our feelings of compassion, encouraged to disbelieve our own knowing that animals suffer.

I am thinking of the many who are still holding their sense of mercy in check for fear of social disapproval. I kept mine in check for too long. And each time I let it out, I felt the pressure to conform—true enough. What helped me? It was seeing others speak out, be ridiculed, and have the courage and inner certainty to speak out again and again. If we can be desensitized to animals' pain, then we can also desensitize ourselves to being ridiculed and pressured.

So I am saying that the more all of us give animals a voice through us, the more courage we give to the millions of merciful people who are already prepared to say, loud and boldly, "Enough! The violence ends here with me right now." Courage begets courage. Thank God for all the heroes that have gone before us and taken a stand. "Nothing is more powerful than an individual acting out their conscience, thus helping bring the collective conscience to life," says Norman Cousins.[20]

The more visible Love becomes,
the more it grows.
Let us all
Be Love
Made visible.

We are actually witnessing the development of our species into *Homo ahimsa*. Yet many of the most dedicated humanitarians remain more or less unaware of the incredible suffering of animals primarily because it is so hidden from view.

An advertisement I saw in a catalog of natural and organic food illustrates this well. Many of the people who order from this catalog are "cultural creatives" dedicated to making the world a better place, and they are very conscientious about what they eat. Yet an ad for Shelton's Poultry appeared in the catalog, obviously intending to elicit a positive response. The ad started by saying, "We were makin' jerky one day, and this cow walked up. . . . He was very upset that we only made Turkey Jerky, when everybody knows that beef is what jerky should be made of." The ad goes on to say that the cow felt that the company was discriminating against him. So in order to placate the cow, the folks at Shelton's decided to develop a new product line of beef jerky. This little ad was, of course, intended to be funny. It is an excellent example of how desensitized loving, intelligent, conscientious people can become to animals. For centuries using animals for our own pleasure has been condoned. The total lack of respect for the cow and the turkey in the ad is anything but funny, but many people will laugh, because it's socially acceptable to do so, and, in fact, expected.

Animal advocates are iconoclasts. Iconoclasts are icon busters. They bring down the icons and challenge the validity of cherished beliefs. Let us listen to some famous iconoclasts:

- *The time will come when men such as I will look upon the murder of animals as they now look upon the murder of men.*
  —Leonardo da Vinci[21]

- *Until one has loved an animal, a part of one's soul remains unawakened.*—Anatole France[22]

- *[T]o love the little creatures is to love God, the great lover of the little ones.*—T.L. Vaswami[23]

- *I have no doubt that it is part of the destiny of the human race, in its gradual improvement, to leave off eating animals.*
  —Henry David Thoreau[24]

- *Compassion, in which all ethics must take root, can only attain its full breadth and depth if it embraces all living creatures and does not limit itself to mankind.*—Albert Schweitzer[25]

- *The love for all living creatures is the most noble attribute of man.*—Charles Darwin[26]

- *Nothing will benefit human health and increase chances for survival of life on Earth as much as the evolution to a vegetarian diet.*
  —Albert Einstein

- *The greatness of a nation and its moral progress can be judged by the way its animals are treated.*—Gandhi[27]

- *Nonviolence leads to the highest ethics, which is the goal of all evolution. Until we stop harming all other living beings, we are still savages.*
  —Thomas Edison[28]

- *The time has come for humans and insects to
  turn toward each other. . . . Such is the way to
  wisdom, the source of our healing, our guidance
  into the twenty-first century.*

  —Thomas Berry[29]

The Evolution of Animal Consciousness
*One early evening, on a hike . . . with Baron,
my German shepherd, he suddenly stopped and
sat down in front of me. . . . He kept looking at
me until I, too, sat down in the grass, and then
he turned away from me and gazed at the set-
ting sun. His eyes fixed to the west, he sat
immobile until a while after the sun had set.
When he came out of his reverie, he nudged me
and we took off again across the meadow, he
playfully, myself in awe.*—Bill Schul[30]

Animals are evolving spiritually along with us, and
indeed all the rest of creation is evolving as well. Allison
Phinney believes that God did not will animals to be violent. He reasons that a Loving God would not have, as
a Divine Plan, the interminable attacking and eating of
one another. He proposes that what we see in the violence of the animal world is not real and lasting.[31] As we
human beings are growing in consciousness, we are
finding new ways of communicating with animals and
understanding their spirituality and their true nature.

Like us, they are made of God's love. Perhaps the vision of the lion lying down with the lamb is precisely the Great Spirit's design. As we send out more and more love to enfold the earth, holy wonders we may not even be able to imagine will begin to unfold.

This concept demands of us that we grow in compassion and that, in that growing and maturing, we and the animals will be elevated in our mutual spirituality.

Penny Patterson, president of the Gorilla Foundation, is the lifelong companion of Koko and Michael, two gorillas who have learned to communicate with sign language. Koko and Michael are changing our world view of animals. They talk with Penny and her staff about feelings that they have that are just like our own. They paint lovely pictures. Michael remembers and can tell the story of his traumatic capture in Africa when he was two years old and his mother was murdered at the hands of his captors.[32]

Chimpanzees at the Georgia State Language Research Center are using a computerized electronic speech synthesizer. By selecting symbols on a keyboard, the chimpanzees can make a statement in electronic English. A mother chimp is teaching her child to use the keyboard, and some chimps are actually copying human speech sounds with their own voices.[33]

Not only are animals growing spiritually themselves, but they are also helping *us* grow spiritually. It's even possible that we may find one day that they are actually ahead of us and leading us ever upward. There is certainly abundant evidence of this. Animals have modeled for us fidelity, nobility, compassion, and love. They have changed peoples' lives and hearts. This poem wonderfully illustrates this:

A Hunter's Poem
A hunter shot at a flock of geese
that flew within his reach.
Two were stopped in their rapid flight
and fell on the sandy beach.
The male bird lay at the water's edge
and just before he died,
He faintly called to his wounded mate
and she dragged herself to his side.
She bent her head and crooned to him
in a way distressed and wild,
Caressing her one and only mate
as a mother would a child.
Then covering him with her broken wing
and gasping with failing breath,
She laid her head against his breast,
a feeble honk . . . then death.
This story is true, though crudely told.
I was the man in this case.
I stood knee-deep in snow and cold,
and the hot tears burned my face.
I buried the birds in the sand where they lay,

wrapped in my hunting coat.
And I threw my gun and belt in the bay,
when I crossed in the open boat.
Hunters will call me a right poor sport
and scoff at the thing I did,
But that day something broke in my heart,
and shoot again? God forbid.

That poem always makes me cry. We bear witness when we cry, when we feel so intensely the pain of another. We honor these geese and that hunter with our tears. Take time to cry. It's important. And breathe. And believe.

I do not know who wrote that poem. I was at an animal rights rally in Kansas City with my children in 1970. This amazing man read his poem into a microphone and everyone I saw was in tears. The poem was distributed without his name. Someday I hope to hear from him so I can give him credit for a poem that has touched so many hearts.

Kinship of Compassion

Stories abound about the altruism shown by animals to each other—including other species, even us, their worst and most violent enemies. Here is a story that was reported recently in *Guideposts* magazine.

Gene Pritchard and his first mate Mark were going down fast in the foggy waters of the Santa Barbara

Channel off the California coast. It was 7 a.m. Their 50-foot shrimp boat was sinking so quickly there was no time to send a distress signal. Luckily the rubber life raft survived the disaster and both men were able to clamber onto it. The floor of the raft was rotted and leaking. Wind and currents were carrying them out into the Pacific. In addition to those odds, the cold water and air threatened them both with deadly hypothermia.

Gene prayed to God to send help. Not long after his prayer he heard a strange whooshing sound in the water nearby. It was the breathing sound of a whale. Thinking she was just passing by, Gene and Mark at first took little notice. But the whale hovered near all day. The fog began to clear at dusk, and the two men got a look at the huge gray whale. Gene wrote: "The whale seemed to look right at me. I felt powerless to look away. As our eyes met, something as vast and certain as the sea itself assured me this great animal was an answer to my prayer."

By morning, after a night of life-threatening cold and storm-tossed waves, instead of finding themselves helplessly drifting in the Pacific, the men heard the sound of surf and felt kelp brushing the bottom of their boat. All night long they had felt the gentle nudgings of the whale as she pushed them back to safety.[34]

This is a story not just of altruistic rescue but also one of tender forgiveness. These were human beings, the species that has brought many nations of whales to the brink of extinction, brutally murdered both parents and children, separated families, and held many whales captive against their will. Yet this whale rescued these men, spent the night patiently escorting them home. She certainly had other things to do and other places to be, but she chose compassion.

There is a further, even deeper mystery in this true story. Gene Pritchard knew that the whale was an answer to his prayer. That means that somehow the whale was listening to and responding to some cosmic communication system. Some might say God sent an angel to rescue Gene and Mark, and the angel was a whale. This mystery is so great that we can only listen in awe and humility to stories such as these.

Another true story tells of a woman who fell overboard in the Indian Ocean. She was literally carried for two full days on the back of a sea turtle until she was rescued by a fishing boat. This turtle neither ate nor dove during the entire rescue. I don't know whether the woman prayed or not, but God is Love, and Love in the form of a beautiful sea turtle came to her rescue and would not leave her until she was lifted from the sea.

A similar story tells of Michael Miller, who, while snorkeling off the island of Hawaii, was caught in a rip tide and carried out to sea. He could not overcome the force of the current. He knew he could not make it back on his own, so he began to meditate. Within minutes, he was surrounded by a group of sea turtles. The biggest one swam underneath him and paused until he could get a handhold on the turtle's shell. This turtle carried Michael all the way to the beach, then turned and swam back out to sea. During their time together, Michael was filled with a sense of peace and a feeling of oneness with all life.[35]

Not only do these stories demonstrate that animals can be altruistic, compassionate, and willing to sacrifice their own comfort to rescue beings from other nations; they also show us that a mysterious kind of communication exists on this earth whereby the Creator and "we" and "they" connect. There are many unanswered questions. How did the whale and the turtle find these people in trouble? Why did they stop to help? Did the Divine tell them to rescue these folks? Or did they just know somehow that they must? How did they even know that the people needed to get to land? Why didn't they just assume that the people were some strange sea creatures that didn't need any help?

And, most provocative of all, could the whale and the turtle be sending us a message through their actions, a simple message of Wisdom that has come to us from the mystics of all religions? The message seems clear and precise: *Let us love one another, for we are all one family.*

Author Bill Schul asks us to ponder the mystery that, although we have killed more than 80 percent of some species of dolphins and continue to kill them, "Yet there is no record of a dolphin ever having injured a person, not even when that person is engaged in killing a dolphin." These beings are certainly more than capable of killing us. Instead, they rescue us, play with us, heal us, and try to communicate with us."[36] Cetacean expert Joan Ocean believes that dolphins and other cetaceans have information for us and want to help us undo the damage we have done and live harmoniously with the earth.[37]

Mark Twain commented that if a man could be crossed with a cat, "it would improve the man, but it would deteriorate the cat."[38] Robert Louis Stevenson is often quoted as saying, "You think dogs will not be in heaven? I tell you, they will be there long before any of us." The Reverend Henry Ward Beecher said, "Happy would it be for thousands of people if they could stand at last before the Judgment Seat and say 'I have loved as truly and I have lived as decently as my dog.' "[39]

In Marshall, Missouri, there stands a life-size bronze statue of Jim the Wonder Dog. Born in 1925 as a Llewellyn setter, Jim lived with Sam and Pearl VanArsdale. He became famous for miles around for his amazing abilities. He foretold Franklin Roosevelt's election and guessed the World Series winners for seven straight years. He could understand instructions in Morse code, shorthand and foreign languages, none of which were known by the VanArsdales.

There are now many books in print and more on the way sharing thousands of true stories of the altruism and highly developed sensitivity animals show to us and to animal nations other than their own. Each one of those books is a beacon of enlightenment showing us all that the animals are our beloved sisters and brothers, and the war against them simply has to end.

Ask the Animals, and They Will Teach You

But ask the animals, and they will teach you, or the birds of the air, and they will tell you . . .
—Job 2:7–10

Animals rescue us, teach us, comfort us, heal us. Companion animals give us their faithful love. Free animals in the wilderness gladden our hearts just by letting us see them. What is it that thrills us so?

As I write this, I am sitting on a boat in San Carlos Bay in Mexico. Off to my right two pelicans just dove head first, wings back, at exactly the same moment about ten feet apart. Two big splashes. Then both bobbed up together, looked at each other, and flew off. Off to my left gulls are soaring on the wind, maybe 20 or 30 feet above the bay, calling to each other, chattering away. Here comes a pelican flying right toward me, wing tips just inches above the water. Then she veers off to the left and looks down at me over her shoulder. I smile and wave. Tears come to my eyes in gratitude for such a gift as that—so close to a wild pelican and eye to eye. Thank you, God. Thank you, Sister Pelican.

There have been many moments in my life in which, by grace, I was privileged to be visited by a wild angel. In 1979 I spent a week among the gray whales at Magdalena Bay in Baja Mexico. The whales gather there early in the year to have their babies and to mate. My companions and I spent most of the days drifting in small wooden boats watching in quiet reverence. We were all enraptured by babies swimming toward us curious to see who we were and by the adults a little farther away holding watch over their youngsters. A sense of holiness purified the whole area; we were guests in the Church of Holy Wonders. It was similar to the time I sat on a stone to watch the sun go down over the Grand Canyon. As others joined me, no one spoke, but each simply found a seat, nodding quietly to the others. The sense of reverence was in each one of us. Being with the whales was similar to that, but I'd have to multiply the reverence factor by maybe 1,000.

One night it was my turn to sleep on a raft anchored out in the Bay. All around me in the dark I could hear the rhythmic breathing of the whales and the lapping of the water against the raft. Then suddenly I heard a "whoosh" just inches from me. I was in my sleeping bag on the very edge of the raft. I reached out my hand and rising up to meet my fingers came a whale. She moved very slowly, gliding along the side of the raft and allowing me to leave my hand on her silky, wet back. I felt as though she were welcoming my caress. For a few moments, we communicated in some fathomless, oceanic way with ancient images and music that rose up out of the sea.

That this great being had allowed me to touch her moved me to tears of awe and joy. I was touching a part of God. I was touching a being so out of my reach, so uncommon to my life, so powerful, and she was touching me too. Thank you, God. Thank you, Sister Whale. I am transformed forever by your gift to me.

We are all in profound and sacred relationship to all the created universe. Anytime a link is made between us and someone of another animal nation, we draw closer to the Divine in us all.

Matthew Fox, at a Kinship with All Life conference in San Francisco, spoke of animals coming into our dreams and into our lives more and more these days. They are trying to reach us, trying to communicate with us through symbols and gestures. We need their help spiritually as much as they need our help on the physical plane. They are trying to tell us that we are here to praise and celebrate life together, not to make war against each other. The very word "anima" means "ensouled one" or "soul."

Are animals evolving spiritually along with us? I believe they draw close to us, as the whale did to me, to help us grow and also to aid in their own spiritual development. I know beyond any doubt that my encounter with Sister Whale transformed me and opened my heart to a grander vision. I sense that she was deeply moved by it as well. We are growing together, inseparable siblings on the journey Home.

Instinct to Love

We know from the many stories told and scientific observations made that animals show love, empathy, and altruism. Many people, including myself, believe they are capable of spiritual ecstasy as well. Companion animals have often been observed enjoying the atmosphere created when human beings meditate. Like Baron, the German Shepherd, chimpanzees have been seen sitting in reverie watching the sun go down.

There are many folks, however, who would prefer to attribute all animal behavior to choiceless instinct. A mother cat will endanger her own life repeatedly to rescue her kittens from danger and move them to a place of safety. A human mother will dive into icy rapids to rescue her child. Is one behavior instinct and the other love? Or perhaps both behaviors are instinct. Suppose for a moment that the instinct to rescue one's offspring is actually a cellular pattern for love. In other words, perhaps, we start out as biological organisms with cellular programming to behave in ways that keeps us and our babies alive. Then as we mature and tune in to spirit, our behaviors can be more definitively called "love." As we enter the realm of mystics who have reached god-realization, we see that their cells vibrate at such a refined level that their love and compassion extend to all creatures, all creation. Gregg Braden exclaims that "our cells are trying to tune into the higher expression of energy" exemplified by Jesus.

Vibration, as we are now learning from scientists, affects form. Emotion is a vibration that can be measured by scientific instruments. Our cells are constantly vibrating to one emotion or another. We can transform our cells willingly and consciously by shifting our experience and belief systems from fear to love. In this way, we emit more love vibrations toward the world, toward other people, toward animals, and toward the earth. Let us expand our instinct to protect our own (which is our instinct for love) out into the universe. Our supreme task in this historic evolutionary leap is to give birth to our own divine nature. This is our second birth, which is true liberation from narrow egotism and fear.

Sharon Callahan, an intuitive animal communication specialist and flower essence practitioner, says she has concluded that animals "come to us in order to draw themselves closer to the Divine." When we are stressed, they experience our stress. When we take time to meditate and pray, they experience peace.

Sharon is one of many researchers who believe animals are here with us to grow spiritually. She tells a story of an Indian saint, Ramana Maharshi, who showed great reverence for the animals who were drawn to his ashram. One was a cow named Lakshmi who would rest her head on Ramana's feet while he sat with his devotees. When Lakshmi was dying, Ramana sat with her and laid his hands on her heart and head. He told his devotees that her heart was filled with love for God and that she had attained enlightenment before she left this realm.

While visiting Japanese Buddhist monasteries, Sharon observed the monks bowing in reverent greeting to all, animals and humans alike. The animals there "are seen as divine beings evolving toward perfect enlightenment just as we are."[40]

We know that St. Francis believed animals had souls and were on a spiritual path. He was often seen preaching to many different kinds of animals. When he spoke to them, they would become quiet and listen intently to him. There are stories of a lamb who followed him around as he preached and fish that would swim up to him when he was near a shore. It is said that at his death, the people attending him saw a large group of larks that swirled around his hut and sang songs to him.

There are a few theologians and students of the Old and New Testaments of the Christian Bible who find support there for the understanding that animals have souls and that they are developing spiritually toward harmlessness and enlightenment along with us.

J.R. Hyland, editor of *Humane Religion*, points out that Genesis verses 1:29, 30 and 2:7, 19, if read in Hebrew, clearly state that animals "were created as 'nefesh chaya'—living souls."

The Creation story of the Bible goes on to say that God made the animals because Adam was lonely. Whether this is read literally or symbolically, the intention is clearly that animals and people would be good companions for each other, not opponents or victims.

The prophet Isaiah declared that in the new world, people and animals would live together in peace in a world in which they would not "learn war anymore" (Isaiah 2:3, 4). At the Phoenix, Tolstoy Farm, and Sabarmati ashrams that Gandhi established, there were many snakes. Because of their dedication to ahimsa, the people chose not to kill any of the snakes, though many of them were poisonous, and there were children in the ashrams. In all the years that they spent there, no one was ever bitten. Gandhi firmly believed that it was because they were living in God's will, in an attitude of peaceful coexistence and mutual respect. Prophecy proved possible.[41]

The ancient Celts and many of the aboriginal peoples understood intuitively that all life depended on mutual harmony. Their relationship to creation was not mechanistic use or even the rather arrogant idea of stewardship. The term "kinship" comes closest to describing the relationship to nature that came naturally to them. Kinship contains within it the idea that we are mutually interdependent; that we all care for each other; that no species is superior to any other. In Celtic tradition, an "anam cara" is a soul friend, someone who loves you just as you are and sees your light and your inner beauty. What a perfect description of animal companions. It is a great blessing to find an anam cara. How many of us have found ours with the dogs and cats and other animals who have come into our lives?

Were We Meant to Be Barbarians?

Were we meant to be the barbarians that we are—to kill each other and animals by the billions, to fear each other, to try to dominate and control one another?

If the Universe is a friendly place and God is a loving God, then—No—we are not meant to be the violent creatures that we are. We are meant to grow, mature, and become creatures of compassion. And in our hearts, deep inside, we know this. Throughout history, there have been people and animals who have shown the other side of our nature—that of selfless compassion.

So we know we are capable of living without violence. We are literally at the helm of this gigantic global ship of consciousness. We can go to port and devolve into more brutality and ultimate destruction, or we can go to starboard and evolve consciously and on purpose into our true nature.

The Tibetans made a choice 1,400 years ago when they chose Buddhism. At that time, they lived as barbarians. They conquered many people in their days of violence. But when they chose to accept Buddhism as a better way to live, they adopted the value of compassion as the central theme of their lives.

Consequently, they destroyed all their weapons and began living in harmony with nature. This required a conscious choosing of a new lifestyle and an ongoing effort to learn throughout their lifetimes how to control their thoughts and actions and to cultivate love, joy, generosity, and compassion.

Robert Thurman, author of *Essential Tibetan Buddhism,* tells us that Tibetans believe we are all potential geniuses and "that the primary evolutionary mandate of human life is for all human beings to cultivate their powers of wisdom, justice, gentleness, loving, and creativity to the maximum degree." The Buddha believed that we human beings are equipped to evolve, if we will choose it, into beings of compassion, genius, and selfless service. He saw these beings that we can become as fully aware of the interconnectedness of all life and fully devoted to respect and care for all creation. To Buddhists, harmlessness and compassion define the lives of those who have awakened and thus been liberated from ignorance. Ignorance results in fear and self-centeredness. When we wake up to wisdom, we *know* our connectedness to all creation and are filled with love and joy for all.[42]

The Prophet in Kahlil Gibran's famous book tells us that we have a "god-self" within us that is perfect. That "god-self" dwells in us along with our humanness. We are evolving toward waking up to our god-selves and leaving behind our limited human attitudes and polarized thinking.

Oftentimes have I heard you speak of one who commits a wrong as though he were not one of you, but a stranger unto you and an intruder upon your world. . . . But I say that even as the holy and the righteous cannot rise beyond the highest which is in each one of you, so the wicked and the weak cannot fall lower than the lowest which is in you also . . . the wrongdoer cannot do wrong without the hidden will of you all. Like a procession you walk together towards your god-self.[43]

Simply put, if we are ever to bring compassion for animals to the world, we must love those who we think are harming them, *and* we must humbly admit that the same impulses and fears that lead them to do harm are lurking in us as well. We are not better than they or more holy. In fact, we are not *not them*. *We* and *they* are one. In truth, there is no difference between us at the level of spirit. As long as we think we are right and good, and they are wrong and bad, we will feed the very fears, hatreds, and violence that we say we want to heal.

We are being called to end violence in thought, word, and deed toward ourselves and toward every person, animal, plant, and the earth herself. We are being called to end the treason against trees, the genocide against the gentle, and all hatred toward each other. We are being called to awaken to our true nature as *Homo ahimsa.*

Chapter Three

THE DIVINE WILL
Love for All Beings

The Elegant Simplicity of the Divine Will
The Divine Will:
In four words: Be Love With Me
In three words: Love One Another
In two words: Love All
In one word: Love
Simply Love

Dr. Martin Luther King, Jr., said, "This Hindu-Muslim-Christian-Jewish-Buddhist belief about ultimate reality is beautifully summed up in the first epistle of Saint John: Let us love one another, for love is God."[1] And as we know, "one anothers" are not just human beings.

God is not "up there" somewhere saying, "I wish they'd hurry up and have world peace. That's what I've wanted all along." God is not frustrated and upset that we're still waging war and eating animals and destroying the environment and thinking, "Why can't they just stop fighting and be nice?"

God is a dynamic energy stream of Pure Unconditional Love that is courting each one of us, wooing us, tantalizing us with moments of epiphany when, for a slice in time, we gasp in wonder at the immensity and power of the Truth. The Truth is that we are one with that energy stream of Love. We are made of It. It is in our every cell. We are one with all creation. Once we understand that fully and completely, we cannot live from anyplace but love. Then, our will becomes the Creator's will; the Divine will; the burning desire for the Highest Good. World peace and reverence for all life are simply natural outcomes of our living in Divinity, visible symptoms of all of us being Love itself.

Our Inner, Higher Will, and Divine Will Are One

And really, isn't our will already aligned with Divine will? Deep within us, we are all spiritually encoded to bring love to earth. This message tends to be enforced in children's films, such as Disney's *The Littlest Horse Thieves*, in which three children rescue the "pit ponies" from a mine when they learn the heartless adults are planning to slaughter the ponies. The theme is repeated in the *Free Willy* movies and many others. The children depicted in the films intuitively know it is wrong to kill, capture, incarcerate, or otherwise harm animals, so they must defy the adults who have lost their sense of mercy and rescue the animals. Movies for older teens, however, no longer feature the rescuing of animals. The focus of many of their movies shifts to horror, explosive action, and a growing desensitization to violence toward animals.

In many ways we could see our own development as a species recapitulated in our development from childhood to adulthood. We start out in the "garden of Eden," where hopefully our needs are met by loving parents and we approach the world with trust and love for all people and creatures.

Yet in the process of developing independence, we must, as individuals and as a species, go through a period where we leave the safety of home behind. This leads us into danger and risk and calls us to invent ways to solve the problems we meet along the way. In the adolescence of our species development, we have found safety in tribes or cliques and looked at those outside our circle as inferior or even as our enemies, slaves, or food.

As individuals we reach adulthood and begin to learn more about interdependence and the need for diplomacy and altruism. We are entering adulthood as a species now. We have left behind the innocence of our infancy, when mother earth fed us directly. We've suffered through the agony of separation from the Creator as we tried, in our adolescent drive for independence, to establish our separate identities. Now, we are entering our cosmic, collective adulthood. We were never separated from the Great Spirit. We just thought we were. And as we surrender to our true nature as interdependent beings, each blessed with unique, individual souls, we turn our faces back toward our old enemies and all those whose suffering we've ignored in our quest to keep ourselves alive, and we say "Ahhh—it's all God, it's all me, we're all one—so beautiful, so sacred."

The flower of Love is growing out of the fertile, composted suffering of us all.

Pierre Teilhard de Chardin said, in an effort to encapsulate God's will in a short sentence, "I became man for you; now you become god for Me."[2]

> *Love all of God's creation, the whole of it and every grain of sand. Love every leaf, every ray of God's light! Love the animals. Love the plants; love everything. If you love everything, you will soon perceive the divine mystery in things. Once you perceive it, you will begin to comprehend it better every day. And you will come at last to love the whole world with an all-embracing love.*—Fyodor Dostoevsky[3]

Yet All Wild Creatures Fly from the Sight of Us

Around the turn of the century, C.W. Leadbeater was reminding people that God's will was for love to be evident among all creatures. No one was to be left out of this circle of compassion and love. Yet, Leadbeater says, "we have brought things to such a pass with our miscalled 'sport' and our wholesale slaughtering, that all wild creatures fly from the sight of us. . . . Is that your idea of the golden age of worldwide kindliness that is to come—a condition when every living thing flees from the face of man because of his murderous instinct? . . . Every one of these creatures which you so ruthlessly murder has its own thoughts and feelings with regard to all this [and] the whole atmosphere around us is full of their horror and pain."[4]

His All Holiness, Bartholomew I, is the Ecumenical Patriarch of 250 million Orthodox Christians. He has been nicknamed the "Green Patriarch" because he has taken a firm stand for environmental protection. He believes it is against God's will to cause species to become extinct and to degrade the earth, acts he considers to be crimes against the sanctity of creation. In 1997, he told a stunned audience at a conference in Santa Barbara, California, that God's will is for us to guard creation and be good stewards. "How we treat the earth and all of its creation defines the relationship that each of us has with God. It is also a barometer of how we view one another." The audience was shocked by such a powerful church leader taking such a strong stand for creation. Bartholomew went on to say, "It is God's gift of love to us, and we must return that love by protecting it and all that is in it."[5]

So What Is the Plan?

If the Creator's will (which is also our true inner will) is simply for love to incarnate, to be made visible, then is there some sort of Divine Plan designed to make it happen? There are many modern-day prophets, channelers, and interpreters of ancient prophecies with lots of ideas and theories. But we don't need to be specially gifted to answer this question. Do we want the world to become more loving and caring or do we want it to become more violent and selfish? Not a very hard question.

I'm not asking, what do we think will happen? I'm asking, what do we want to happen? Well, I'm just going to bet very heavily that the majority, if they knew they had a choice, would vote for more love, care, and compassion.

Why would we vote that way? It is because we, you and I, are the Divine. The Divine lives and breathes in us. "The Kingdom of Heaven is within." Or, as the Indian saint Ravidas said, "Under the vast vault of blue lives the divinity clothed in hide."[6] We are the sacred bubbles in the vast ocean of the Divine, each one of us aspects of the Creator God. Our true and highest will and God's will are one and the same.

Our own interior, intuitive wish for the earth is love. We got that wish from our Creator, who is Love. We are here to make it happen.

Would it make any sense to say that we are supposed to evolve into creatures that are *more* cruel and *more* violent? Would it make any sense to say that God's will or the Divine purpose is for all of creation to continue to suffer when we are free to choose to stop the suffering?

The New Testament tells the story of Saul who later took a new name and became known as the disciple Paul. Saul was a well-known agent of death to Christians. He had murdered many of them because of their beliefs. One day he was walking along the road to Damascus when Jesus appeared to him as a blinding light. As the story goes, Saul was blinded, then healed, and came to believe in Jesus' teachings. He gave up killing and began to teach about love.

We human beings are on our "road to Damascus" now. There can be no doubt that we are being asked to leave the killing behind and change our names from *Homo sapiens* to *Homo ahimsa*.

You can see that I am answering this question about the Divine Plan in an ultra-simplistic manner. There are many different seers and futurists with much more complex scenarios of what our future holds for us. I leave it to them to fill in the blanks, and we can all use our own imaginations as well. But for the purpose of this book, I prefer to take aim at one simple, one single goal—Love. If we do that, if we stay focused, laser-like, on that one bright star, everything else will fall into place, as we choose, act, feel, think, pray, and be love. Calvin DeWitt, a pioneer in the Christian "creation care" movement, asks us to see "all creatures through God's eyes, beholding the beauty of the Beholder."[7]

Religious fundamentalists and extremists of most faiths tend to see God as vengeful and violent. They believe that if they perform the correct rituals (much like a child in fear of an abusive parent) that they will be spared the wrath of God while the nonbelievers will be punished. Mystics, on the other hand, the God-intoxicated ones, who live in intimate relationship with the Creator, have discovered that God is unconditionally loving of all people, all animals, and all creation regardless of what they do or believe. It is the mystics who remind us that God's will is that we *all* love each other and live in peace. St. Basil the Great, a mystic of the fourth century, once said,

> *I want creation to penetrate you with so much admiration that wherever you go, the least plant may bring you a clear remembrance of the Creator. . . . One blade of grass or one speck of dust is enough to occupy your entire mind in beholding the art with which it has been made.*

Not One Sparrow Is Forgotten

Veterinarian and author Mark Walters tells the story of Herb Kale, an ornithologist with the Florida Audubon Society. Herb had studied the dusky seaside sparrow (which is now extinct) for decades and had helped care for the last sparrow of the species until she died in captivity June 15, 1987. Kale seemed unaffected by the death until a friend opened his heart with an epitaph for the little bird. The epitaph read,

To think that a necklace would
never miss one of its pearls,
Or a song one of its notes,
Neither this spring, nor ever again,
Will your exuberant performances appear
On nature's stage.

Upon reading those lines, the formerly unmoved Kale sobbed with grief. He later told Walters, "Memories of my sparrow will ride the final beat of my heart."[8] Not one sparrow is forgotten by God (Luke 12:6). This is Divine will that we be moved to tears for our passionate love of life longing to live.

How are we to build a new humanity?
Reverence for life. Existence depends more on
reverence for life than the law or the prophets.
                    —Author Unknown

One of the most often repeated prayers among Christians is the Lord's Prayer. There is a phrase in that prayer that holds a key to understanding the Divine Will. It goes like this, "Thy kingdom come, Thy will be done in earth as it is in Heaven." Jesus and mystics of all religions make it very clear that the kingdom of heaven is within each of us. In other words, each one of us holds the potential of Heaven within us. We are each capable of manifesting it in the outer world. We are the builders of paradise here on earth. Gandhi talked about bringing heaven to earth. He commented that if we could "erase the 'I's' and 'mine's' from religion, politics, economics, etc., we should soon be free and bring heaven upon earth."

Every time the Lord's Prayer and similar prayers from other religions are recited, people are praying, whether they know it or not, for an end to the torture and killing of animals.

Altruistic Hippos Bring Heaven to Earth

All the animals who have, throughout history, been sacrificed, tortured, slaughtered, and confined by people have died and made their transition to the next realm as the pure spirits that they are. Just as we have done, they came to earth as spirits to inhabit physical bodies. We all come to experience the beauty of earth and to make whatever effort we can to reach a higher expression of love—not just us, the animals too.

Two hippos could give us all lessons in cross-species altruism. The first was witnessed and photographed by Dick Reucassel for *Life* magazine. This hippo saw a young impala being attacked by a crocodile. The hippo charged the crocodile, who let go of the impala and swam away. But the impala was badly hurt, so the hippo nudged her up onto dry land, guarded and licked her, and even tried to help her to stand up.[9]

Harry Erwee, a researcher in Zimbabwe, and other witnesses saw an impala being chased through the water by a pack of wild African dogs. A nearby hippopotamus, observing this, decided to intervene, swam to the impala and nudged and guided the exhausted animal away from the dogs. The hippo literally pushed the impala, who was by now shivering uncontrollably, onto dry land. Then, to the amazement of the human observers, the hippo opened his huge mouth and "repeatedly breathed life into the animal until it regained its strength and ran off."[10] Who knows how many other stories there are to tell about hippo heroism that humans haven't witnessed?

I read a story once about a medical student who was diligently cutting open a living, breathing dog to study his beating heart. The dog gazed at him, awake, with a look of absolute trust and love. That look awakened, or, perhaps, reawakened, something deep and true in this young man. He suddenly became appalled at what he was doing (much like Saul on the road to Damascus). From that day forward, he refused to harm innocent animals. He had looked into the eyes of Unconditional Love and been transformed.

Could it be possible that that dog incarnated for the specific purpose of sacrificing himself (like Jesus and others) in the hands of the young man in order to teach him about the sacredness of all life in one single loving gaze? Perhaps we cannot say definitively "yes." But we certainly can't say definitively "no" either. It's possible. Dogs and many other animals have given their lives willingly for others more times than can ever be counted or even known, because so many of these events take place without being observed by human beings.

Mother Teresa used to say that the sick and dying she cared for did more for her than she did for them. They were teaching her compassion. It's possible that this is the mission of these animals as well.

So perhaps we can find some peace in our hearts knowing that the animals who have suffered and died at our hands are at peace now. And, perhaps, through their death, they reached someone and turned their thoughts toward compassion, toward the possibility of kinship with all of life. It is through moments of connection such as these that darkness becomes light and pain becomes joy, for we are indeed all family.

The Divine Plan Is Heaven Here on Earth

We have talked of God's will being that love be manifested, made visible everywhere. This "outpicturing" of Love is Heaven on earth. It is a great waking up to the cosmic holiness in each of us. How it will all manifest once we reach this next stage of our evolution is beyond anything we could design or pray for by ourselves. Therein lies the awesome power of our faith, as we surrender to the Cosmic Architect and trust that the

"Highest Good" we pray for is better than anything we could design alone.

We know that our negative thoughts have manifested a world in a lot of pain, and as we have matured, we have come to realize that we can now create a world of beauty, truth, and love by changing our thoughts, our actions, and our expectations. "As a man thinketh so is he." As humanity thinketh, so *is* the world. Thich Nhat Hanh says, "Earth will be safe when we feel in us enough safety."[11]

Thomas Merton declares that the whole universe depends on our hope and vision, "Because our hope is the pledge of a new heaven and a new earth, in which all things will be what they were meant to be. They [all life] will rise, together with us, in Christ. The beasts and trees will one day share with us a new creation and we will see them as God sees them and know that they are very good."[12]

"Thou shalt not kill" does not apply to murder of one's own kind only, but to all living beings, and this commandment was inscribed in the human breast long before it was proclaimed from Sinai.—Leo Tolstoy[13]

The Divine will is Love. We are instruments of that Love. We breathe It in from God and we breathe It out to all that is. The more we do that, the closer we get to

God realization, which is Love realization, which is full awareness. And, as Ram Dass says, "The end of suffering [for all beings] is full awareness."[14] The Holy Will of us all is a world without cruelty, a world embraced in the Circle of Infinite Compassion.

Chapter Four

SACRIFICE, CRUCIFIXION, AND RESURRECTION OF THE ANIMALS

For I desire compassion and not sacrifice.
—Matthew 12:7

Gandhi, St. Francis, and Jesus Rescue Animals from Sacrifice

While visiting Calcutta in 1901 Gandhi wanted to see the Temple of Kali. On the way he noticed a long line of sheep being herded toward the Temple. When he arrived at the entrance he recoiled in horror. "We were greeted by rivers of blood. I could not bear to stand there. I have never forgotten that sight."

Later that evening, a friend tried to console Gandhi by telling him the sheep felt no pain. But he knew better and spoke out vehemently, saying that the barbaric custom should be abolished. He wrote of this painful memory, "To my mind the life of a lamb is no less precious than that of a human being. I should be unwilling to take the life of a lamb for the sake of the human body. I hold that the more helpless a creature, the more entitled it is to protection by man from the cruelty of man."

Gandhi longed for the terrible practice of Kali sacrifice to stop, but he felt that he was not pure enough for the task. He prayed for someone to emerge, "some great spirit, man or woman, fired with divine pity, who will deliver us from this heinous sin, save the lives of the innocent creatures, and purify the temple."[1]

In St. Francis's time, sheep were also sacrificed by ignorant Christians who thought they were somehow honoring the crucifixion, which was the "sacrifice" of the Lamb of God—Jesus. Whenever Francis discovered that this practice was about to take place, he rescued the lambs and tried to teach the people that killing innocent animals was not a path to God.[2]

Jesus himself stopped the "moneychangers" from selling doves and other animals for sacrifice right in the temple itself. All the Gospels—Matthew, Mark, Luke, and John—tell this important story. Jesus, normally peaceful and loving, was enraged by the selling of sheep, cattle, and doves for the purpose of sacrifice. "So he made a whip of cords and drove all from the Temple area" (John 2:13). Reverend J.R. Hyland considers this the action that led to Jesus' crucifixion. Hyland explains that the religious leaders in Jerusalem tolerated preachers and reformers like Jesus. It was not his words that caused them to want to be rid of him but his disruption of the profitable selling of animals.

This event took place as people were preparing for Passover, a time when thousands of animals were sacrificed. This ritual had become quite an economic mainstay of the city. "In trying to end the slaughter of animals, he (Jesus) was attacking the economic foundation of Jerusalem," Reverend Hyland explains. The sacrifice, which could only take place in the Temple, brought in tourists (known as pilgrims then) and made money for artisans, craftsmen, farmers, and the politicians.

The day that Jesus committed this very public act was the 10th of Nisan. This was the day that men arrived at the Temple to select the animals they would kill. The killing would begin at 3 p.m. and continue in three shifts with 6,000 people killing 6,000 animals in each shift. At the end of the killing approximately 18,000 animals would be dead. Each man would carry an animal into the Temple and line up in a row across from a row of priests. At a signal, the men would slit the throats of the animals. The priests would catch the blood in buckets. These buckets of blood were then passed along a line and thrown against the altar.

In the midst of this, the terrified animals screamed and urinated and defecated in fear. Imagine the smell, the sounds of screaming, and the rivers of blood. Centuries before, the prophet Isaiah had conveyed a message from God to the people of Jerusalem making it quite clear that God had "had enough of burnt offerings of rams, and the fat of fed cattle, and I take no pleasure in the blood of bulls, lambs, or goats. . . . Your hands are full of bloodshed. Wash yourselves, make yourselves clean" (Isaiah 1:11, 15, 16). Jesus said he came to fulfill Isaiah's prophecy. Therefore, it was necessary for him to directly confront this idolatrous "worship."

Four days after Jesus freed the animals, he himself was crucified in what has become known as the sacrifice of the Lamb of God. Hyland believes his crucifixion was in direct retaliation for his interference with the Passover sacrifice of thousands of animals.[3]

> *The true God is love, goodness and mercy, not sacrifice, cruelty, killing, and murder. . . . We shall not kill or sacrifice other creatures for him; we shall only sacrifice ourselves for our human and animal brothers.*
> —Reverend Carl A. Skriver, 1977[4]

Sacrifice to the Gods of Money and Power; Crucifixion of the Innocents of Earth

Religious sacrifice continues to this day, although it is widely condemned as useless and meaningless by many modern churches. Yet many of the very people who condemn ritual sacrifice in churches condone the ritual sacrifice of animals in slaughterhouses, scientific laboratories, fur farms, the pet trade, animal entertainment, and many other modern "temples."

The verb "sacrifice" is defined by Webster as "to offer to a god or deity in homage or propitiation." Today the sacrifice of animals to the gods of money, science, medicine, appetite, and power has expanded beyond belief. Our earth is a holy temple. Our bodies are holy temples. The animals' bodies are holy temples. There are rivers of blood everywhere.

Crucifixion has the specific meaning of the torturing and killing of the innocent Jesus by nailing him to the cross. The verb "crucify" also has a more general meaning, that is, to subdue completely, to torture, torment, and to treat cruelly. If the general human population could see behind the walls of the millions of human institutions dedicated to the sacrifice and crucifixion of billions of innocent animals as well as nature herself, they would see the violence the human race has embraced to create luxury, pleasure, and power.

But because so much of the violence is not visible to the general public, most people live in the illusion that many of the products they buy are good for them. They do not know the enormous price that was paid by the animals, the water, the forests, and the starving children for the hamburgers they eat and the clothes they wear.

The Good People Who Don't Yet Understand

A good example of this lack of knowing is an article in the Christian publication *Focus on the Family* (September, 2000) that profiled S. Truett Cathy, founder and CEO of Chick-fil-A restaurants. In the article, he is described as "a doer of the word," a man who has "built a business empire by putting people first." Mr. Cathy is a kind, loving, and very successful man. He has taught Sunday school classes for teenage boys for 45 years. His own sons are executives in his company. In the segregation days of 1948 in Georgia, Cathy defied convention and hired an African-American, named Eddie White. Eddie says that Cathy "was like a second father to me." Cathy also founded a foster home system, a summer camp, and a scholarship foundation.

He is a master entrepreneur. He started out with one tiny restaurant and now owns nearly 1,000 Chick-fil-A restaurants in 35 states. His spiritual beliefs are evident in his business. Rather than offering children Disney trinkets with their meals, he offers premiums for Christian-oriented books and videos. His corporate purpose is "to glorify God by being a faithful steward of all that is entrusted to us." He also keeps his restaurants closed on Sundays.

Cathy is a highly respected man and a humanitarian. He is filled with faith in God and a determination to do the right thing. But his spiritual practice begins and ends with people. He lives, as does the majority of people on earth today, with the conviction that animals are for our use, that they have no sovereignty of their own and that their suffering is of no consequence to us, if indeed it even exists. My rough guess would be that over

15 million chickens are slaughtered every year just for
Mr. Cathy's restaurants alone if he sells 50 chickens per
day in each restaurant, 6 days per week. That's just a
guess, and I have tried to be conservative.

In one advertising campaign, Chick-fil-A shows a
toy cow carrying a sign that says "Eat mor chikin."
(Evidently, this cow disagrees with the cow mentioned
earlier in this book who was jealous of the turkey who
got to be made into jerky.) The advertisers are assuming
that consumers would think it cute to anthropomor-
phize a cow for the sake of selling more chicken, but
would refuse to consider that cows (and, of course,
chickens) suffer just as we do.[5]

I have put Mr. Cathy in the spotlight here, because
he is such a wonderful example of the many dedicated,
spiritual, generous, loving people who are our brothers
and sisters, but who are completely in denial about the
horrific violence that, behind the scenes, supports their
businesses. How long would Chick-fil-A restaurants last
if the continuous slaughter line of 15 million chickens
was part of the restaurants and visible to all the cus-
tomers when they came in to place their orders?

For centuries, this violence has been condoned, and
people, in general, are desensitized by generations of
meat eating and animal cruelty that is simply accepted
as normal and necessary. It is also seen as beneficial. By
sacrificing the voiceless and the helpless to the gods of
money and power, millions of people have reaped the

blessings of those gods. Torturing and killing innocent creatures pays big bucks in the short run, but the cosmic debt that accrues moment by moment is unfathomable. As Albert Schweitzer admonished, "No one may shut his eyes and think that the pain, which is not visible, does not exist."

Mr. Cathy, and so many others like him, have done great things for people. They deserve our respect and admiration for their good intentions, generosity, love of people, and hard work. They do not know, really know, what they are doing. It is our job to help them, in as loving a way as we can, to see the truth that Jesus, Gandhi, St. Francis, and others taught—that the Divine Will is for compassion, not sacrifice. We are to love one another, all "anothers," not just the human ones.

Chicken Soup for the What?

Another example of the extreme and radical desensitization of humanity to animal cruelty is the tremendous popularity of the best-selling series of *Chicken Soup for the Soul* books. In these books, hundreds of heartwarming stories are gathered under the "chicken soup" title, thus linking the slaughter of innocent chickens with sweet stories of love and friendship. These books are all excellent and have blessed the lives of millions of people. I highly recommend them. I only wish the editors had given them titles consistent with their aim of making the world a happier place. I subtitled this book *Veggie Soup for the Chicken's Soul* to help us all awaken from this worldwide slumber in which we simply do not notice the degradation and disrespect of animals contained in commonly heard phrases.

Gandhi taught that our souls and our bodies cannot find healing at the expense of another's suffering. His ten-year-old son, Manilal, once developed typhoid and pneumonia. The doctor ordered that Manilal be given eggs and chicken soup, but Gandhi had taken the vow of ahimsa (harmlessness). He had promised God that he would do no harm to anyone. What was he to do? "I told him," Gandhi related in his autobiography, "that we were all vegetarians and that I could not possibly give either of these two things to my son." So he asked for alternatives, but the doctor could offer none.

Manilal himself refused the eggs and chicken soup as well. "I will not have eggs or chicken broth," he said to his father. Together they proceeded in faith. After much alternative therapy and prayer, Manilal recovered and was, at the time the story was written, "the healthiest of my boys." Gandhi concluded, "There should be a limit even to the means of keeping ourselves alive. Even for life itself, we may not do certain things."[6]

St. Francis was struggling with an illness that didn't seem to be getting any better. A nobleman who loved and admired Francis sent him a living pheasant, thinking it would make a healing soup for Francis to eat. Instead of eating him, however, St. Francis was overjoyed just to be near the beautiful bird, and they became great friends. Francis was often heard saying to the bird, "Praised be our Creator, Brother Pheasant!"[7]

Oh Jerusalem . . . how often I have longed to gather your children together as a hen gathers her chicks under her wings.—Matthew 23:37

Sacrifice in the Holy Temple of Mother Earth: Statistics

Here is a small glimpse into the sheer immensity of human-caused suffering to animals and the earth:

- According to the USDA National Agricultural Statistics Service over 9.8 billion land animals were killed for food in the U.S. alone in 2001—including 41.6 million cattle and calves, 118 million pigs, 4.2 million sheep and lambs, 8.9 billion "broiler" chickens, 450 million laying hens, 390 million turkeys, and 27.7 million ducks. Worldwide, nearly 48 billion land animals—8 times the human population of the world—were killed for human consumption, according to the U.N. Food and Agriculture Organization.[8] These figures do not include the horses, foals, dogs, cats, and wild animals killed, or the millions of male chicks who are ground up and thrown away.

- Fish are measured in tons rather than as individuals. According to the Worldwatch Institute, 89 million tons of fish individuals were caught and killed worldwide in 2000.[9] The number of individuals would easily be in the billions. Tragically, 27 million tons of the marine animals caught, including marine mammals, were killed and discarded as useless.[10] This means, for example, that 20 pounds of ocean beings are killed for every pound of shrimp eaten.[11] Fifty percent of the remaining marine animals were fed to livestock.[12]

- The average American meat eater consumes 2,450 chickens, 118 turkeys, 33 pigs and sheep, and 12 cattle and calves in one lifetime.[13] This is amazing when one considers that our bodies are not designed to be carnivorous.

- Factory farms generate 2.7 trillion pounds of manure per year and have polluted 35,000 miles of rivers in 22 states and contaminated ground water in at least 17 states.[14] This contamination is compounded by the many deadly chemicals also contained in factory farm runoff.

- One pound of meat requires 2,500 gallons of water to produce. A pound of wheat takes only 25 gallons.[15] There would be no hungry people in a world of vegans, who consume no animal products of any kind.

- One acre of land can produce either 165 pounds of dead cow meat or 20,000 pounds of potatoes.[16]
- 125,000 square miles of rainforest are destroyed every year just to raise cattle. This is in addition to all the forests destroyed for lumber, rayon, and paper.[17]
- Every year in the U.S., hunters kill 45 million mourning doves, 30 million squirrels, 28 million quails, 25 million rabbits, 20 million pheasants, 14 million ducks, 6 million deer, and thousands of geese, bears, moose, elk, antelope, swans, cougars, turkeys, wolves, foxes, coyotes, bobcats, boars, and others. Millions more are crippled, orphaned, and terrorized.[18]
- "The two major causes of extinction are hunting and destruction of habitat," according to the Senate Committee on Commerce.[19]
- Hunters pay to shoot exotic animals in private, fenced shooting preserves. These are called "canned hunts." Other forms of "sport" hunting include: "contest kills," in which shooters use live animals as targets in front of cheering crowds; "wing shooting," in which hunters use mourning doves for target practice and leave 20 percent crippled and unretrieved; "baiting," in which hunters attract bears, deer, and others to piles of food and then shoot them at point blank

range; and "hounding," in which dogs with radio collars are used to find and corner animals until the hunters can follow the radio signal and shoot the terrified animals.[20]

- Because hunting is declining in popularity (perhaps because most people really don't like hands-on killing), the U.S. Fish and Wildlife Service and half of our state wildlife agencies are sponsoring youth recruitment programs to get children and women interested in hunting.[21]

- Each year the egg industry starves millions of hens for up to 14 days to force them to molt. Ninety-eight percent of all hens used for egg production are painfully debeaked and crammed in groups of 5 or 6 into tiny cages so small they cannot move about normally.[22]

- Only 2 out of 10 kittens born in the U.S. ever find a lifelong home. sixty-four percent of animals who arrive at U.S. shelters are killed. That's more than 10,000 cats and dogs killed each day.[23]

- Almost two-thirds of all large mammal species are threatened or endangered in the lower 48 states.[24]

- A 40-inch fur coat requires the skins of 16 coyotes or 18 lynx, or 60 minks, or 20 otters, or 40 raccoons, or 8 seals, or 15 beavers.[25]

- In the U.S. alone, 27 million animals each year are tortured in research, testing, and education. Sixty thousand of those are primates.[26]
- Over 75,000 mares are cruelly confined and kept pregnant in order that their urine can be collected to produce the hormone replacement drug Premarin. The majority of their foals are sold for slaughter.[27]
- Dairy cows are cruelly confined in intensive milking operations. Their babies are taken from them at birth and many are fed low-quality milk, kept in tiny stalls, and slaughtered for veal at 6 to 8 weeks of age.[28]
- The number of insects that are killed for human convenience each year exceeds our ability to count.

People remember two world wars in the twentieth century. Animals count one long unending world war against their unarmed nations. If there were a war memorial wall that named each individual animal killed just in their twentieth-century war, no one would have to travel far to pay homage or bring flowers, for the wall would stretch across America from sea to sea many times.

Just as religious people around the world have sacrificed animals in hopes of pleasing their gods, canceling out their sins, and bringing them good fortune, human beings around the planet now sacrifice animals to bring themselves what they believe will be good health, entertainment, good clothing, money, and all kinds of pleasures. Implicit in this activity is that human good fortune is of greater value than the lives and freedoms of these animals, these other nations of beings. Author Jon Wynne-Tyson comments,

> [I]n our half-baked thinking and incessant ferocity towards the countless sentient creatures whom, alive, we imprison, mutilate, maim, trap, strangle, shoot, hook, chase, snare, de-limb, behead, suffocate, flay, disembowel, stab, crush, force-feed, burn, drown, boil, freeze, cut up, make sick, terrorize and by numerous other means mercilessly exploit day in and day out for no better reason than that we wish to devour them, we are shamefully forsaking that one obligation which, above all others, we should recognize—to put our unique knowledge of the difference between good and evil, between mercy and cruelty, before our heart-hardening greed.[29]

The Suffering of the Animals Is Our Suffering

Paramahansa Yogananda said that wars are not caused by God or fate but rather by "widespread material selfishness." Such greed emits subtle negative rays. The cumulative effect of these negative energy emissions "disturbs the electrical balance of nature." This brings disasters upon us all.[30] Imagine what powerful negative and destructive energies are being charged every moment as the wars against innocent animals continue to rage on.

Most religions regard hell not as a place of punishment, but as an internal sense of being separated from God. In actuality, we cannot be separated from God, because the Divine dwells in all things. But we can surely feel such separation and cosmic loneliness. When human beings cut themselves off from the realization that nature and animals are sacred and endowed with the very being of the Creator, they cut themselves off, often unknowingly, from the full experience of oneness with God and the inner peace and bliss that accompany that oneness.

That is why the Bhagavad Gita says that those who are nonviolent to all creatures are "dearest to God." The more compassion we have in our hearts for all beings, the closer we feel to the Creator, because all beings are manifestations of the Divine Energy of Compassion. That is why St. Bonaventure said that every creature is a "likeness of the eternal Wisdom."[31]

So all this crucifying and sacrificing that is taking place, this war upon the animal kingdoms, is hurting more than the animals. All of the greed, neglect, cruelty, and disrespect perpetrated against them is reflected back to all the perpetrators. The spiritual atmosphere of our earth is heavily polluted with the groaning and suffering of billions of beings who just want to live.

> *Whenever we cause suffering or death to any other being, we cause suffering to the Great Life Force.*—Shik Po Chih[32]

Martyred Animals and Resurrection
There is something profoundly Christ-like about the innocent suffering of creatures who have done no harm and who are utterly dependent upon our mercies.

—Reverend Andrew Linzey[33]

Reverend Andrew Linzey, an Anglican priest who is calling the churches to a new and higher ethic of concern and compassion for animals, says that animals are "litmus tests of our Christian compassion." Jesus is portrayed as a lamb in the scriptures, an image that conveys his defenselessness and innocence in the face of those who crucified him. This calls out a sense of mercy from within us for one who is unfairly tortured and killed. The Christiaan cross is a symbol of the suffering of those who are innocent and whose sanctity is not fully known.[34]

Christiaan Barnard, the world-famous heart surgeon, kept two male chimpanzees in separate cages. His plan was to sacrifice one of them and transplant his heart into a human being. While the team was preparing the chimpanzee for the transplant, the chimp cried a great deal. After he was taken from his cage and killed, the other chimpanzee wept bitterly and was inconsolable for many days. After this sad experience, Dr. Barnard "vowed never again to experiment with such sensitive creatures."[35]

If the poet Robert Browning had been the intended recipient of the heart, he would have refused. He once said, "I would rather submit to the worst of deaths . . . than have a single dog or cat tortured to death on the pretense of sparing me a twinge or two." Robert would have been enthusiastically joined by Gandhi and St. Francis, I'm sure. Evidently, Mark Twain would also have joined their ranks. He said he did not care whether or not vivisection produced results that helped humanity; "The pain which it inflicts on unconsenting animals is the basis of my enmity toward it."[36] He saw no need to look any further for reasons to end the practice. Andrew Linzey asks us to see the face of Christ in the millions of animals suffering in factory farms, laboratories and slaughterhouses, and in animals hunted for sport.[37]

The good news about crucifixion of the innocents is that there is always resurrection. Indeed, our stories and myths of martyrs and heroes demand of us the hope of resurrection. The spirit of the chimpanzee that Dr.

Barnard killed was resurrected in the physician's new-found compassion.

The farm animals sacrificed to the gods of greed and appetite are resurrected every time another person takes the vow of veganism or ahimsa. The spirits of the horses who have suffered and died so drug companies could grow fat on the sales of Premarin are resurrected every time another woman tells her doctor she will never take Premarin.

Sharon Callahan, the animal communication specialist mentioned earlier in this book, writes that animals who are suffering in terrible conditions "have told me that they offer themselves willingly if just one person is touched by their plight and motivated to change."[38]

In my meditations, I have come to understand that as well. Many animals are quite advanced souls who have incarnated in animal bodies with the sole intent of teaching and service. They know that we will reach a point (which is now) when enough people will teach the world through photographs, films, books, lectures, demonstrations, vigils, songs, and prayers about the extent of the killing that is taking place. The secrets behind the curtains and doors of circuses, labs, slaughterhouses, and other dungeons of torture are being revealed. Hearts are being thawed, consciousness is being raised. Some of the animals are literally martyring themselves, because they know that eventually the shock of what humanity is doing will awaken enough people to the tragedy and it will be forever terminated.

This is not such a far fetched idea when we consider the multitude of stories about animals who have given up or risked their lives to save their human and animal friends. I am reminded of the St. Bernard who had the misfortune of being disliked by a very cruel man. This man tied a heavy weight around the dog's neck and pushed him into a raging river. As he pushed, however, he lost his own balance and fell in. The St. Bernard, who was fully aware that this man had just tried to kill him, in spite of the weight around his own neck, turned toward the drowning man and rescued him from the river. Needless to say, this man experienced a resurrection of love in his own heart. It is in such ways that darkness becomes light and pain is transfigured into joy.

Jesus' crucifixion and death was a sacrifice designed to teach the ultimate truth that we must forgive and *love one another*. His spirit is resurrected in each one of us when we are able to stop violence and love and forgive. The spirits of the animals are resurrected in each one of us when we awaken and end the violence toward them.

The animal nations are making their own dramatic contributions to the evolution of ahimsa consciousness. Let us join with them on an energetic and spiritual level to encourage them and give them hope. They are not alone and we are not alone in the struggle. We have them; they have us; the people perpetuating the violence have our love and prayers; and we all have the Divine energy rushing in to embrace us. Shadows of violence fade in the presence of this brilliant beacon of love.

Chapter Five

HOMO AHIMSA
The Next Giant Step for Humanity

By ethical conduct toward all creatures, we enter into a spiritual relationship with the universe.—Albert Schweitzer

Ahimsa: The Highest Expression of God Realization
When we start out as baby souls on our spiritual paths, we do many cruel and selfish things. Sometimes our worst mistakes and darkest hours become the catalysts for our discovery of sacred truth, because we find that, in spite of our behavior, the arms of the Loving Universe are always open, welcoming us into ecstatic experiences of oneness with God. It is often these little ecstasies that build our faith and draw us into the foothills of our journey to God realization. But as we begin the ascent into the mountains of cosmic consciousness, we find that the transformation we long for requires of us a deeper fusion with the infinite, a dedication known as ahimsa.

If we eat the flesh of living creatures, we are destroying the seeds of compassion.
—Buddhist Surangama Sutra

Ahimsa is a Sanskrit word meaning "noninjury." It is common to Buddhism, Jainism, and Hinduism, but, as we shall see, it is an ethical principle and spiritual practice available to anyone, regardless of religion or philosophy.

Ahimsa is the highest expression of God realization. It is where we are all headed as a species if enough of us turn the tiller and set our sails in that direction. It is the natural expression of one who has discovered the truth, regardless of their religion or background. As Albert Schweitzer said, "Any religion which is not based on a respect for life is not a true religion or philosophy."

The Rich Meaning of Ahimsa

Ahimsa is a word rich with meaning. Over the centuries, it has come to mean more than noninjury. In an effort to get at its essence people have described it as:

- Selfless service
- Confronting violence with love
- Turning the other cheek
- Universal, pure, divine love; agape
- Cosmic awareness of the interconnectedness of all life

- Nonviolence
- Harmlessness
- Reverence for all life
- Compassion and sympathy for all life

A more specific translation of ahimsa is the "abstinence from causing any pain or harm whatsoever to any living creature, either by thought, word, or deed," according to Sri Swami Sivananda.[1] It is the central theme of the Jain religion of India, which is one of the oldest religions in the world. The Jains say, "Master of his senses and avoiding wrong, one should do no harm to any living being, neither by thoughts nor words nor acts."

The Five Point Plan for Jain Ecology

The Jains offer a "Five Point Plan for Jain Ecology" as a contribution to solving the major problems of the world. They propose that if we follow these five points, we will create a world in which all life can peacefully coexist. Their points are:

1. "Nonviolence in Thought, Speech, and Action." This involves praying, thinking, talking, and acting in ways that bring health, peace, and prosperity to all beings. This includes caring for deserted animals, feeding ants, rodents, dogs, and others, and rescuing animals bound for slaughter by buying them.

2. "Avoiding Wastes." Jains discourage wasting water, utilities, fuel, paper, clothing, food, etc. This helps reduce garbage, which helps the environment, and encourages us to share with the less fortunate.

3. "Non-Acquisitiveness." Any surplus beyond one's basic needs and plans for old age should be shared with those in need.

4. "Vegetarianism." Killing a five-sensed animal is the highest sin in the Jain scriptures. The Jain diet is designed to inflict "minimum injury on one-sensed life only [plants], which is necessary for sustaining our bodies." Thus, animals are not killed, and much less land is needed to sustain human beings on a vegetarian diet. Although Jains have traditionally included dairy in their diets, the advent of cruelty in dairies has caused many of them to eliminate dairy from their diets and from their religious rituals.[2]

5. "Charities and Donations." Jains encourage giving away what we do not need to causes such as health research, illiteracy, animal rights, unemployment, devastation of forests, pollution, and prevention of animal sacrifice, to name a few. This beautiful plan ends with a prayer:

*May the noble and sublime principles of
Jainism permeate our hearts for a better tomorrow in which reverence for all life will be
intensely nurtured. Om, Shanti, Shanti, Shanti.*[3]

Ahimsa: Path to Spiritual Bliss

Gandhi and many of his students took the vow of ahimsa. Ahimsa is both an ethic of conduct and a path to
spiritual bliss. Tolstoy said, "If a man aspires towards a
righteous life, his first act of abstinence is from injury to
animals."

The reason that ahimsa is the ultimate spiritual
path is that, as the Avatamsaka Sutra says, "Each object
in the world is not merely itself, but involves every other
object and, in fact, is everything else." Therefore, to
inflict harm on any being, we harm ourselves and we
harm that which is holy and divine.

*Mercy is a universal duty, and it cannot be
withheld from any of God's creatures.*
—Reverend Humphrey Primatt, d. 1790[4]

Ahimsa is the ultimate goal of all human beings,
religious or not and regardless of religious affiliation.
Jesus, Buddha, St. Francis, Gandhi, Martin Luther
King, Jr., Albert Schweitzer and many others modeled
ahimsa for us, though they may have used different
terms to describe what they were doing.

Deep in our hearts we know that harmlessness and nonviolence are better than harm, suffering, pain, and violence. But the vast majority of us have relegated ahimsa to the realm of saints and God's "chosen few." We have believed that ahimsa was too difficult for ordinary folks to attain. Perhaps we have believed that we had to have special powers to live a life of harmlessness, selfless service, and universal love.

But this is a new day.

There is ahimsa in the air.

By the grace of the Creator within, we are becoming *Homo ahimsa*. All the violence we have engaged in up to now has been against our divine nature.

> . . . *and as by [God's] breath the flame of life was kindled in all animal and sensitive creatures, to say we love God as unseen and at the same time exercise cruelty toward the least creature moving by [God's] life, or by life derived from [God] was a contradiction in itself.*
> —John Woolman[5]

Long ago, Plutarch wondered how the first human meat eater could possibly have ever "touched his mouth to gore and brought his lips to the flesh of a dead creature." How could he, he asked, have "set forth tables of dead, stale bodies and ventured to call food and nourishment the parts that had little before bellowed and cried, moved and lived"? He wondered how human beings could have ever managed to endure the sight and the stench of killing, and how they could have thought it proper to slaughter the harmless, tame animals that "Nature appears to have produced for their beauty and grace. . . . No," he declares, "for the sake of a little flesh we deprive them of sun, of light, of the duration of life to which they are entitled by birth and being."[6]

Mark Twain seemed to be dialoguing with Plutarch when he said, "Of all the animals, man is the only one that is cruel. He is the only one that inflicts pain for the pleasure of doing it."

Schopenhauer adds that the common human assumption that animals have no rights and that there are no consequences to our cruelty toward them "is a positively outrageous example of Western crudity and barbarity. Universal compassion is the only guarantee of morality."[7]

Universal compassion is our destiny, our highest spiritual calling. We can choose ahimsa now as a global ethic, or continue on toward global destruction. Let us believe that not only you and I, but all of us, can be transformed by the renewing of our minds (see Romans 12:2) and the renewing of our hearts.

Sri Swami Sivananda, a Hindu spiritual teacher, states unequivocally that "Ultimate Truth can be attained only through ahimsa," and "No self-realization is possible without ahimsa."[8] Gandhi stated emphatically, "The only means for the realization of Truth [and God is Truth] is ahimsa."[9]

Ahimsa is not a duty or a rule. Ahimsa is both a means to obtaining inner bliss and a result of obtaining inner bliss. In other words, if we commit to lives of ahimsa and practice it daily in what we eat, think, purchase, say, and do, then we are continually practicing being conscious of our interrelatedness with all creation. The more we practice being aware of that, the more it becomes part of us. The more it becomes part of us, the more we are filled with joy as we come to recognize the truth and wonder of who we are and how we are all living together in this great sacred sea of Divine Love.

So ahimsa is a means to obtaining inner bliss through ahimsa behavior and consciousness. It is also the result of inner bliss. That is because once we begin to experience the inner bliss of our God connection, we can behave in no other way. Once we begin to live large parts of our days blissfully aware of our own personal connection to God and all creation, it becomes unthinkable to do harm to another, because we are filled with love for it all and because we see clearly that everything we do affects every other being. If we want this to be a loving world, we can do nothing less than to love all, for the Great Spirit, as Black Elk says, is within all things.[10]

Beyond Personal Bliss to Global Compassion

So the benefits of ahimsa are both personal, for it brings joy to each practitioner, and global, for the love and compassion we practice have a harmonizing effect on all of creation.

Another way of understanding the spiritual benefits of ahimsa is to recall the ancient law of cause and effect, "As a man soweth [in thought, word, or deed], that also shall he reap" (Galatians 6:7). This is also known as karma and is a fact taught in nearly every religion and philosophy in the world. Ahimsa sows the thoughts, words, and deeds of compassion, forgiveness, mercy, harmlessness, truth, and love. By practicing ahimsa, that is exactly what we will reap.

There is a story about a wandering saddhu who was so in tune with the Divine energy and so conscious of the holiness all around him that whenever he sat down to rest, a shrine sprang up out of the ground at his feet.

Wherever I am is holy ground; wherever you stand is holy ground; the land of all creatures is sacred. Gandhi said, "God is even in these stones."[11] Gandhi is in the stones, as am I, as are you. The essence of God is in everything. Heaven is already *in* earth waiting to be revealed. Harming or destroying that which is sacred (and everything is) sows seeds of destruction. Of course, we are reaping the harvest of that harm now on a global scale. Protecting and loving that which is sacred sows the seeds of creation. Through ahimsa we will reap the rewards of beauty, peace, and love within ourselves and for the world.

Violence Begets Violence and Love Begets Love

Very simply—violence begets violence and love begets love. If we continue to eat and wear our friends, use cosmetics and medicines that are tested on them, support circuses, rodeos, and other forms of entertainment where they are abused, and all the other common activities so condoned by mainstream thinking, then we perpetuate massive, worldwide violence. This perpetuation is delaying our development. It is delaying the reaping of the fruit of love. We cannot "practice random acts of kindness" to humans while continuing to support the slaughterhouses and dairies and expect to have world peace.

> *We are not ashamed to sacrifice a multitude of other lives in decorating the perishable body and trying to prolong its existence for a few fleeting moments with the result that we kill ourselves, both body and soul.* —Gandhi[12]

> *Personally, I would not give a fig for any man's religion whose horse, cat, or dog does not feel its benefits. . . . It is now our bounden duty to abolish the futile and ferocious oppression of those creatures of our common Father which share with man the mystery of life.*
> —Reverend Dr. S. Parkes Cadman

St. Francis, Jesus, Buddha, Gandhi, Albert
Schweitzer, and Jane Goodall commune with the Divine
and know the bliss that comes with experiencing the
oneness of all life. All of them are famous for their compassion and love, not just for human beings, but for all
creation as well.

Kasturbai Gandhi, like her husband Mohandas
Gandhi, took the vow of ahimsa. One day, following a
surgical operation, she was very weak. Her physician
feared for her life. He told Gandhi she must drink beef
tea, and if Gandhi refused to permit it, the doctor would
then refuse to treat her any further. Gandhi discussed
the matter with Kasturbai, fully intending that, if she
wanted to drink the tea, then he would support her
decision. But Kasturbai was determined. "I will not take
beef tea," she said. "I would rather die in your arms
than pollute my body with such abominations." Gandhi
carried Kasturbai that very day to the train station. She
regained her strength at home giving thanks to God and
not to "beef tea."[13]

When we think of ahimsa as universal love, we
understand it as a universal ethic not confined to any
one religion or philosophy. Most mystics who have
experienced ecstatic union with God and with all life
are also not confined to any one religion or philosophy.
Though some, like Saint Francis of Assisi, may remain
true to their religious roots in some ways, in other ways
they are thorns in the sides of the church because of

their insistence on the simplicity of Truth. Dogma, religious politics, hierarchical systems, and complicated rituals are superfluous to them. The Truth is so simple. Love one another. That's it. Ahimsa is simply the experience and the action that comes forth from living the "Love one another" ethic.

The wisdom of ahimsa and harmlessness embraces all of creation in that ethic. This is what we are being called to do now as a people. Whenever we hear discussions or prayers or admonitions to "love one another" or to "pray for peace for all humanity," let us be the ones to remember and remind others that our love and our peace must encircle all life, not just human life.

Unless the self expands to cover the entire creation of God, there can be no permanent peace.—Kirpal Singh

Ahimsa: A Powerful Tool for Social Change
We have talked about ahimsa as a way of life that leads to God realization, inner peace, and world peace. There is also much to be learned about ahimsa with regard to our direct dealings with people who are cruel to animals. It is a powerful tool for social change. Gandhi and Martin Luther King, Jr. used its principles in their civil disobedience activities. Saint Francis of Assisi, although possibly unaware of the term, nevertheless lived by ahimsa and changed many people's attitudes toward animals in his unique way.

Gandhi called ahimsa "soul force" and also "love force."[14] One who lives by it accepts insults, criticism and even attacks without retaliation or offensive reaction. No matter what others do to provoke the ahimsa sage, the sage never thinks of his or her attacker with anything but love. "Ahimsa is the perfection of forgiveness," says Swami Sivananda. This, of course, takes enormous inner strength, fearlessness, and self-love. Why self-love? Because true self-love is born when we realize that we are all part of God, and so if we attack another being, we are attacking God and we are attacking ourselves.

Gandhi and King taught their students to stand firm when protesting an injustice and never retaliate or engage in violence. Through their teachings, they shed a bright light on the effectiveness of ahimsa. Mother Teresa taught her students the very same principles. "Let us conquer the world with our love," she would say.

King once said that "Gandhi was probably the first person in history to lift the love ethic of Jesus above mere interaction between individuals to a powerful and effective social force on a large scale." He felt that Gandhi's ahimsa practice was the tool of liberation for oppressed people everywhere. It is an equally invaluable tool for the liberation of oppressed animals everywhere.

As he studied Gandhi's philosophy King came to understand that Gandhi was practicing not "nonresistance to evil, but nonviolent resistance to evil."

Gandhi's ahimsa and satyagraha modeled for us all "a courageous confrontation of evil by the power of love, in the faith that it is better to be the recipient of violence rather than the inflicter of it, since the latter only multiplies the existence of violence and bitterness in the universe."[15]

Martin Luther King, Jr.'s Six Facts about Nonviolent Resistance

From his deep studies of Gandhi and his own experience, King developed a list of six facts to help people understand nonviolent resistance and join with him in his vision.

1. Nonviolent resistance is not for cowards. It is not a quiet, passive acceptance of evil. One is passive and nonviolent physically, but very active spiritually, always seeking ways to persuade the opponent of advantages to the way of love, cooperation, and peace.
2. The goal is not to defeat or humiliate the opponent but rather to win him or her over to understanding new ways to create cooperation and community.
3. The nonviolent resister attacks the forces of evil, not the people who are engaged in injustice. As King said in Montgomery, "We are out to defeat injustice and not white persons who may be unjust."

4. The nonviolent resister accepts suffering without retaliating; accepts violence, but never commits it. Gandhi said, "Rivers of blood may have to flow before we gain our freedom, but it must be our blood." Gandhi and King both understood that suffering by activists had the mysterious power of converting opponents who would otherwise refuse to listen.

5. In nonviolent resistance, one learns to avoid physical violence toward others and also learns to love the opponents with "agape" or unconditional love—which is love given not for what one will receive in return, but for the sake of love alone. It is God flowing through the human heart. Agape is ahimsa. "Along the way of life, someone must have sense enough and morality enough to cut off the chain of hate," said King.

6. Nonviolent resistance is based on the belief that the universe is just. There is God or a creative force that is moving us toward universal love and wholeness continually. Therefore, all our work for justice will bear fruit—the fruit of love, peace, and justice for all beings everywhere.[16]

The Alchemy of Ahimsa

Swami Sivananda tells the story of Jayadeva, author of the *Gita-Govinda*. A group of men cut off Jayadeva's hands. Not only did he give them gifts, but he also "obtained Mukti (spiritual liberation) for them through his sincere prayers."[17]

A thief entered the cottage of Pavahari Baba to steal what he could. When Pavahari Baba returned home and saw the thief, he ran after him offering him more, pleading with him to come back and get all that he needed. In awe of this response, the thief never stole again and became a disciple of Pavahari.[18]

This brings to mind the intense moment in the great French novel *Les Misérables,* when Jean Valjean, newly released from prison, finds himself a guest in the home of the Bishop. Jean gets out of bed in the middle of the night, packs the silverware into his bag, and steals away into the night. Jean later arouses suspicion in the police. They detain him and find the silver in his bag. Of course, they drag him back to the Bishop, certain he has stolen the silver. We readers of the tale are caught in the grip of fear that Jean will be sent back to the terrible prison, but to our shock and surprise, the Bishop tells the police that he gave Jean the silverware, and that, furthermore, Jean forgot the silver candlesticks. At that astonishing moment, he hands Jean the valuable objects and, as the police leave, whispers to Jean, "With this silver . . . I ransomed you from fear and hatred."

Closer to home, perhaps, is a true story told by Louis Lehman about his father. Louis was a child at the time. He and his siblings were settled into the back seat of the family car and on the way to church when they spotted a neighbor (a man suspected by many to be a thief) helping himself to the corn out of the family's corn crib. Louis's father stopped the car, and the children wondered what he would say. Their father approached the man, who thought for certain he was in for trouble. Instead, Mr. Lehman said to him, "If that's not enough, come back tomorrow. Take as much as you need. Remember you're my neighbor." The thief was never known to steal again after that day.[19]

Such noble behavior is not outside our grasp. We have within us the seeds of such perfect love. Swami Sivananda advises us, once we set ahimsa as a conscious goal, to begin by controlling our speech and body first. Each day, determine to utter no harmful words and to do no physical harm to any being. By controlling ourselves in this way, we lay the groundwork for controlling our thoughts. While in the beginning, keeping our thoughts always on Love for all is a discipline, eventually it becomes second nature. And with that comes the greatest reward of all, for when we feel unconditional love for all creation, we enjoy the Bliss of God in every fiber of our being.

So not only does ahimsa lead to a world of kindness and compassion for all, but it also brings each one of us into transcendent joy, divine bliss, and non-dual consciousness.

Jesus said in the Sermon on the Mount:

You have heard that it was said "An eye for an eye, and a tooth for a tooth." But I say to you, do not resist him who is evil; but whoever slaps you on your right cheek, turn to him the other also. And if any one wants to sue you, and take your shirt, let him have your coat also. . . . You have heard that it was said "You shall love your neighbor, and hate your enemy." But I say to you, love your enemies and pray for those who persecute you . . . —Matthew 5: 38–40, 43–44

Jesus was teaching people 2,000 years ago that they were on an evolutionary path, leaving the old ways of revenge and violence behind and learning a new way of being. He was teaching how to go beyond concepts of good and evil and to love everyone just as God does. He was teaching people how to express their innate god nature.

Would a god fight back or refuse to offer her coat? And why would she not? Because there is no lack of coats, and there is no thing or person to fear. Not really. Not when you live in Love.

Another reason Jesus would have us turn the other cheek as Gandhi and Pavahari Baba, Martin Luther King, and Louis Lehman's father did so gracefully is because it transforms the aggressor. When we stand fearlessly and lovingly in the face of our attackers, we astonish them. They may still react according to their programmed patterns, but they will be moved by our strength, by our devotion to nonviolence, and a little tiny seed of transformation will be planted. Perhaps we personally will not see the results in that person in this lifetime, but we are assured by those who have gone before us that ahimsa love is the force that will bring heaven to earth.

Tools for the *Homo Ahimsa*

Swami Sivananda gives us this powerful tool. When someone attacks you or your ideas, say to yourself, "He is a baby-soul. He is ignorant. That is why he has done it."[20] Jesus demonstrated that on the cross when he said, "Father, forgive them, for they know not what they do."

Here is another tool. The Divine Spirit of Love dwells in us all. We are all manifestations of the One Mighty Creator, beloved and adored, all of us—from the tiniest one-celled creatures and stones to the giant blue whale. When we hate or injure another being, we are injuring and hating ourselves. Let us see ourselves in everyone. Let us see God in everyone. When we see the Sacred in everyone and everything, we are seeing the true and the real. When anyone commits evil, cruel, and violent acts, they are behaving in that way out of ignorance and fear. They are, at least at that moment, lost and completely unaware that we are all brothers and sisters and that they themselves are filled with the Divine nature.

Yet another tool is this. Remember that in practicing ahimsa, we are totally in sync with the universe and with Divine will. Violence is out of sync. When you are in sync with the universe, miracles happen. All Heaven rushes to your aid.

No greater power exists on earth than this ahimsa or unconditional love. Swami Sivananda says that the law of ahimsa is exact and just as scientific as the law of gravity. "You must know the correct way to apply it intelligently and with scientific accuracy. If you are able to apply it with exactitude and precision you can work wonders." Wonders are needed everywhere for the animals. Let us become wonder workers!

Perfect Ahimsa Is the Ideal

Having said all that, we must accept one thing. Perfect ahimsa on the physical plane is the ideal vision to hold in our hearts, but it's not possible to never cause harm. When we walk and sit, no matter how hard we try, we unintentionally step on and kill tiny beings that lie in our path. Even within our own bodies, antibodies rush to kill invading bacteria. When we eat vegetables and fruit, we may be causing harm. I'm sure everyone would agree that it is not possible to never have an angry thought toward anyone.

People write living wills these days to make certain they are not kept alive artificially when there is no hope of regaining health. When their wishes are honored and life support systems are removed, death is the result. Ahimsa teachers tell us that intention is the key. If the intention is to relieve suffering or to prevent suffering and not to harm, that is crucial.

Gandhi understood and practiced ahimsa as well as anyone ever has. Yet he agrees with Sivananda that even the most devoted follower of ahimsa commits himsa or harm by breathing, eating, and so forth. Also, because we are all tied together in the unity of life, when others commit himsa, the harm they do is done by us as well.

This underlines the importance of growing spiritually and the value our spiritual growth has to the rest of life. It is the motive in our hearts that matters. I know I am speaking to people who love animals. That puts you at the pinnacle of spiritual awareness. Animals and nature are the most maligned and tortured beings on the planet. Those of you who speak out for them and love them endure much criticism and even hatred. It takes enormous strength not only to endure the heartbreak of witnessing the outrageous violence toward the natural world, but also to publicly refuse to participate in it. That strength comes from an inner knowing that love for all is the truth that will set the animals and all of us free.

Gandhi says, "A votary of ahimsa remains true to his faith if the spring of all his actions is compassion, if he shuns to the best of his ability the destruction of the tiniest creature, tries to save it, and thus incessantly strives to be free from the deadly coil of himsa."[21]

Ahimsa: The Hope of the Ages and Our Evolutionary Destiny

Ahimsa or universal cosmic love is to me the hope of the ages and our evolutionary destiny. If we can manage to transform ourselves from the most destructive species on planet earth, it will be because enough of us made a conscious choice to awaken to our true nature. That true nature is ahimsa. That true nature is harmlessness, nonviolence, and unconditional love.

Our false nature encourages soldiers to kill, scientists to torture, politicians to disregard the sanctity of life, men and women to enslave animals and people, and children to participate in the slaughter of millions of helpless animals for food and clothing. Our false nature is created in fear and lack of faith in the abundant goodness of the universe.

Our true nature knows that we are all interconnected, that love is the only thing that is real and everlasting, and that the universe is rich with love, joy, gentleness, compassion, and care.

"To see the universal and all-pervading Spirit of Truth face to face one must be able to love the meanest of creatures as oneself," wrote Gandhi. He was ever humble and never claimed to be a perfect practitioner of ahimsa, but he adored it and set his soul upon it as his highest dream. "I must reduce myself to zero," he said and put "myself last among [my] fellow creatures." But do not think that Gandhi was talking about disappearing into the woodwork. His ahimsa battle cry was ever, "I shall resist organized tyranny to the uttermost."[22]

The Essenes may not have known the word ahimsa in their day, but they certainly understood its principles. The Essenes were a group of families and individuals who lived prior to and during Jesus' time. The influence of their teachings is profoundly evident in Jesus' life. According to the Dead Sea Scrolls which were discovered in 1947, the Essenes did not believe in killing human beings or animals. They refused to sacrifice animals or eat them. They believed that spiritual liberation and joy could only be obtained if people were kind and loving to all God's creation.[23]

St. Francis: Ahimsa Saint

Had he known the term *ahimsa*, St. Francis, the well known thirteenth-century saint of Assisi, Italy, would very likely have said, "Yes, I'm into that." He called it his "marriage to Lady Poverty." This marriage contained the same virtues as ahimsa: forgiveness, humility, nonresistance, selfless service, harmlessness, and universal love. And, of course, it led to the same result for the practitioner: union with Perfect Love, blissful awareness of our interconnectedness with all creation, and a contagious effect of joy and peace on anyone passing nearby.

Although marrying Lady Poverty sounds ascetic and painful, it actually led to the great discovery that the universe is a bountiful, generous, loving place. It is the living out of the Bible verse "Seek ye first the kingdom of God and all these things shall be added unto you." As one of Francis's biographers, Lawrence Cunningham put it, "Living purely in the providence of God and after the manner of Christ's self-emptying, one's awareness of the world as gift is sharpened."[24]

Francis is probably most often thought of in his role as protector of animals. His love for people was certainly just as evident, but, because he was so outspoken for the rights of animals and because that was so rare in his day, the image of him with birds on his shoulder has become a shining symbol of compassion. Francis was often heard to say that people ought to feed the birds corn and other grains.

Francis's life goal was to live a life as much like that of Jesus as he could. So to him it was perfectly natural to show love and compassion for all God's creation. He sought continually to make himself (like Gandhi did) "a zero," a servant of the poorest and most helpless. The animals certainly fit into that category.

Unlike many ascetics of his day who sought to purify themselves for God through penance and self-punishment, St. Francis was filled with joy and an overwhelming gratitude for all the things of nature that God had created. So to him being "a zero" was not a result of self-loathing or punishment but rather the pinnacle of giving oneself in love to one's fellow beings.

St. Francis saw God and the presence of Christ in all the created world. He thanked God for Brother Sun, Sister Moon, Brother Wind, Sister Water, and Mother Earth in his famous "Canticle of Brother Sun." He had a cicada friend at one time who would come to him whenever he called her. He was seen preaching to fields of flowers and telling them to praise God. He spoke often to fields of grain and grapes and to stones and springs of water. He had a clear, unbending recognition of the interrelationship of all created beings to each other and of the necessity that love rule those relations. He saw that we have a mutual responsibility to each other, including the animals and all of nature.[25]

> *If you have men who will exclude any of God's creatures from the shelter of compassion and pity, you will have men who will deal likewise with their fellow man.*—St. Francis of Assisi[26]

One of the favorite stories about St. Francis and his love for animals is the story about the wolf of Gubbio. St. Francis was staying in a town called Gubbio, where it happened that the entire populace was living in fear of a ferocious wolf who was attacking many of the animals that they kept. The people were convinced that the wolf would kill any man, but St. Francis went to find the wolf anyway. With total trust in God, he went into the forest and found the wolf. Instead of attacking St. Francis, the wolf sensed the saint's love and walked right up to him. Francis told the wolf he understood that he was hungry but that he was frightening the people, and that wasn't right. He asked the wolf if he would agree to be kind and gentle if the people of Gubbio would feed him. The wolf agreed by putting his right paw in Francis' hand.

Together they walked back to the town and Francis told the large gathering of people about the wolf's promise. All the people agreed to feed the wolf every day. At that, the wolf bowed and again gave his paw to St. Francis as a sign of his pledge. The people and the wolf lived in peace from that day on and kept their agreement until the wolf died of old age.[27]

Like Gandhi, St. Francis of Assisi lived and taught that we must love and respect all beings regardless of their station in life or how they treat us. Most especially we must love, care for, and humble ourselves before the helpless, including the animals who are the most helpless of all.

If St. Francis came across a person who had less than he did, he would take off his own clothes (which were all he had) in order that he could serve the poor person. His radical desire and joy in poverty did not come from a desire to practice self-punishment or asceticism. Rather his motives were to remove all ownership of things, for he believed ownership caused divisions between people; to live as Jesus lived; and to trust God to take care of all his basic needs. He truly believed that we could all live as God intended and as the universe is designed. That is, we could all live as beings of love, giving love to all creation.[28]

Francis, like Gandhi, taught his students, "To everyone who approaches, be they friend or enemy, robber or highwayman, receive them with kindness." He asked them all to carry peace in their hearts. "Let no one be provoked by us to anger or scandal, but rather let all, through your gentleness be led to peace, tranquility, and agreement."[29]

Francis looked beyond "good" and "evil" as all who have achieved spiritual liberation are able to do. He and his Franciscan brothers and sisters won people over, not through condemnation and fear, but through kindness, respect, and belief that healing takes place in an atmosphere of love. His strategy, to quote Leonard Boff, one of his biographers, was "liberation through kindness."[30]

Whenever there is a violent confrontation taking place, the temptation is to see one side as "good" and/or "victim" and the other as "evil." Gandhi, Francis, and other peacemakers see beyond that. The strategy is not to take sides or judge who is right or who should surrender or compromise.

The strategy is to apply enough love and powerful, radical, unexpected kindness and respect that the opponents are changed at the heart level. In that way they come toward each other to embrace in peace, not because they agree but because they finally recognize that they are each others' kin, endowed with innate goodness.

Again and again we are told by those with heart wisdom to love our enemies. This is ahimsa. This is loving kindness. Resisting anything shuts doors. Ahimsa opens them. The more we can involve ourselves with animal issues in the manner modeled for us by Gandhi, St. Francis, and other vision keepers, the more progress we can make.

> To *him who is joined to all the living there is hope.*—Ecclesiastes 9:4

Learning to Love the Perpetrators of Violence

We are drawn to animals, to love them and care for them, each for our own reasons. This is a calling as lovely and holy as all callings of compassion. But sometimes our love for the animals is counterweighted by our anger at the perpetrators of cruelty toward animals. Whether they be the local elementary school that refuses to offer vegetarian options or an animal testing laboratory, all the people that we are confronting are our brothers and sisters. We are just as intimately connected to them as we are to the animals. If we have angry, hateful, and violent thoughts toward them, these thoughts perpetuate the very vibrations of violence on earth that we want to transform.

Learning to love those who do violence to innocent beings is a lifelong spiritual journey, certainly not an easy task, and I am not saying we must all wake up tomorrow morning transformed into little Saint Francises. But I am asking us to become conscious of our infinite human potential to *love one another* and progressively get better and better at it. While we are expanding the circle of compassion that Schweitzer talks about, we are including everyone in that circle.

And we must also include ourselves in that circle. We must have compassion for ourselves when we explode in anger and disbelief at the endless litany of ongoing cruelties in this world. We must forgive ourselves when we realize that we are sometimes cruel—perhaps to a co-worker, a telemarketer, a spouse, a parent or friend—and that we also participate in the world's cruelty. We need to allow ourselves the full range of human emotions and have faith that we are growing day by day. As we integrate our own anger and fear together with our passion for kindness and love, we achieve a paradoxical union within ourselves. It is a union that keeps us humbly aware of our temptations and shortcomings. It is a union that helps us to find the common ground upon which we all stand.

This is the deeper meaning of the "Beauty and the Beast" metaphor. (The "beast" represents a mythical monster, not an animal.) Our personal challenge is to embrace both the beauty (our own higher self) and the beast (our anger, hatred, and fear) that dwell within us. In this atmosphere of love and acceptance for ourselves, we become one whole and healed entity (living "happily ever after" so to speak). This is also the deeper meaning of the "lion lying down with the lamb" metaphor. As the lion within us lies down and makes peace with the lamb within us, so that there is no fear or struggle between them, then we experience profound inner peace (symbolized by the innocent lamb) united with confidence and empowerment (symbolized by the lion).

Thus is your healing everything the world requires, that it may be healed. The resurrection of the world awaits your healing and your happiness, that you may demonstrate the healing of the world.—Course in Miracles[31]

The great peacemakers all agree that we cannot and do not change others directly. We can only change ourselves from within. If we want to create a loving and compassionate world for the animals, we need to be continually transforming ourselves into loving and compassionate beings.

Veganism as a Gift and a Prayer in Action
There is little hope of abolishing the manifold cruelties to animals which disgrace our society, until men give up the habit of eating flesh.
—Rev. Basil Wrighton, 1965[32]

One of the most compassionate gifts we can give the animals, the earth, and all people is to become vegan. Living a vegan life is nearly synonymous with ahimsa. Vegans use absolutely no parts of any animals in what they eat, wear, or use in any aspect of their lives. Their diet includes no meat, eggs, fish, or dairy products. They do not take vitamins that come in gelatin capsules or contain stearates (which come from the slaughterhouse). Clothing is chosen so that no animals are harmed in its manufacture. This means no silk, wool, rayon (which is made from destroying rainforest habitat), leather, down feathers, fur, or anything else that causes harm to an animal. Shampoos, soaps, beauty products, etc. must be carefully chosen to be sure that they have been produced without animal testing and without any animal ingredients. A 1997 Roper Poll estimated that there were between 500,000 and two million vegans in the U.S.

Veganism is more than a healthy way to live. It is a sacrament, an act of reverence for all life. And, as Nobel Prize winner Isaac Bashevis Singer, said, it is a protest. "This is my protest," said Singer, "against the conduct of the world. To be a vegetarian is to disagree . . . with the course of things. Nuclear power, starvation, cruelty—we must make a statement against these things. Vegetarianism is my statement."[33]

Like ahimsa, veganism is a critical and necessary step on the path of spiritual awakening. The Law of Attraction says we attract to ourselves the energy fields that we radiate. When we eat meat and buy products that have resulted in animal suffering, we participate in that suffering to such an extent that the anguish of the animals becomes part of us. Much of the depression and anxiety so common in the world today, not to mention the many meat- and dairy-related diseases, are a direct result of eating and wearing someone's pain and death. We literally attract back to ourselves, in the form of human diseases and environmental disasters, the violence we have caused to the animals.

The American Dietetic Association reports that vegetarians have a lower risk of heart disease, stroke, colon cancer, osteoporosis, diabetes milletus, obesity, kidney stones, gallstones, hypertension, and breast cancer than non-vegetarians. Vegetarians include dairy products in their diets. Vegans, who do not eat dairy, have even lower risks of these diseases than vegetarians.[34] Louisiana State University researchers reported in the journal *Circulation* that they studied a number of bodies of teenagers and young adults who had died from accidents, suicide, and murder. They found that more than 20 percent of the individuals' arteries were clogged so badly that heart attacks appeared to be an imminent possibility.[35]

Neal D. Barnard, M.D., President of the Physicians Committee for Responsible Medicine, is often quoted as saying, "The beef industry has contributed to more American deaths than all the wars of this century, all natural disasters, and all automobile accidents combined." A study of young American soldiers killed in the Korean war showed clear signs of heart disease as compared with the Korean soldiers, who were primarily vegetarians and had no such signs. Jon Wynne-Tyson's book *Food for the Future* is an excellent source of information regarding our physical incompatibility with meat eating.[36] But these diseases are more than just physical results of eating animals. They are also spiritual results, because it weakens the soul to participate in another's suffering.

Ralph Waldo Emerson once said, "You have just dined, and however scrupulously the slaughterhouse is concealed in the graceful distance of miles, there is complicity."[37] It is this complicity that infects us totally—body, mind, and spirit. Every atom of our beings is invaded by the cruelty which, though hidden, yet cries out in our cells for mercy. Veganism is the ultimate gift, therefore, not only to the animals but to ourselves. As George Bernard Shaw famously said, "Animals are my friends, and I don't eat my friends."

What do we gain by eating meat? A sense of power—that we are on top of the food chain, or maybe even outside of it; that our lives are more important than the animals' lives, so they must sacrifice their lives for us; that they are "just meat," as one young man said to me. There is a thoughtform in our world that encourages the idea that eating meat makes us somehow better than all the rest of creation. But in such thinking, we belie the fact that we are terrified of being like the animals and of being vulnerable to attack as they are. By killing and eating and using them however we like, we prove our tremendous power over them. But of what earthly or heavenly use is power without compassion? One who wields such power without mercy does so at one's own peril and to the detriment of the whole world. Wynne-Tyson points out that we can choose "to learn to live symbiotically instead of like parasites and rogue predators who kill without need or even hatred." He finds no "parallel in nature to mankind's cruelty," which is "the cause of the major ills of our society."[38]

Val Plumwood knows what it's like to be food. She was attacked and almost eaten by a crocodile. The crocodile dragged her into the water and rolled her numerous times before she was finally able to escape. She survived the ferocious attack through her own strength and grim determination. Because of her experience, Val is uniquely qualified to speak of the intimate relationship between human beings and nature. Defending the crocodile, whom many wanted to kill in retaliation for the attack, Val asks how we can believe that we are somehow above the food chain, that we can eat anyone, but no one can eat us. "The idea of human prey threatens the dualistic vision of human mastery in which we humans manipulate nature from outside, as predators, but never prey," she says. So we kill animals by the billions, and this serves to reinforce our idea of ourselves as somehow safe and outside the food chain. We can never be food, but the lives of billions of animals "can be utterly distorted in the service of this end."

"We are edible," entreats Val, "but we are also much more than edible." And it is only just and fair to say that "any creature can make the same claim to be more than just food."[39] We are not masters of nature. We only wish we were, because we fear it. The truth is much more beautiful and enticing. We are an integral, intimate part of nature. It is us, and we are it. We cannot separate ourselves from it. As we try to dominate and destroy it to establish our power, we find that we are destroying ourselves and our earth home and our relations, because we are all connected. But it is the realization of this mystical connection, once fully embraced, that is the key to bringing heaven and peace to earth.

This illusory power that is gained from thinking that people are outside the food chain may be one of the main causes that so many people eat meat. We are certainly not equipped physically, as carnivores are, to attack, kill, and devour animals. We don't have the teeth, claws, or strength for it. We literally and figuratively do not have the stomach for killing. We ask others to do it for us, out of sight, out of smell. And we do not have the short intestines necessary for the proper digestion and elimination of meat. Nor do we find raw meat tasty. We have to cook it and disguise it with sauces and seasonings.

> *I refuse to eat animals because I cannot nourish myself by the sufferings and by the death of other creatures. I refuse to do so, because I suffered so painfully myself that I can feel the pains of others by recalling my own sufferings.*
>
> —German pacifist Edgar Kupfer,
> written while imprisoned in Dachau[40]

The plant kingdom is different from us animals in a very mystical way. The difference is in the fruit. The fruits we bear as animals are our actions. Our art, music, teaching, and acts of kindness are our fruits. When someone devours our teaching or our art, we hope that he or she is spiritually nourished by it. These fruits do not resemble us physically. They are not our physical children. Instead they resemble us metaphysically. They are the children of our imaginations. A song can lift a thousand hearts. One act of compassion can inspire many more.

By contrast, fruit trees, vegetable vines and plants, nut trees, and grain plants grow physical fruits, hold and nourish them on their vines and branches, and then drop them on the ground, all ripe and beautiful. Their beauty attracts animals who brush up against the plant and scatter the seeds, or eat the fruits and then eliminate the seeds in their excrement. The excrement itself nourishes the seed and helps it to grow. This natural cycle of life giving life and continuing to live is an astonishing miracle to me, a metaphor for love and proof of the genius and goodness of the universe.

By contrast, animals are not the "fruit" of their parents. And none of us can grow things on our limbs that look very different from us, drop off of us, and then grow little replicas of us out of the soil as a plant can do. If we eat a cow or a person, we do not defecate out little cow- and people-seeds that are nourished by our manure. When we eat someone's body, we terminate his or her ability to be fruitful altogether. The fruits of animals, such as acts of kindness, are like the fruits of plants only in one way. They are meant to be given away. But that is the only similarity. Plants give away their physical fruit and continue to live and bear more fruit. Animals cannot give away their physical bodies and continue to live.

So veganism is a sacrament, a gift to the animals and to the environment, a protest, a daily prayer—and it is also the bedrock of spiritual bliss. The Buddha said,

"To become vegetarian is to step into the stream which leads to nirvana." Ramalinga Swami, an enlightened master who lived and taught in India in the 1800s, ate only a little rice two or three times a week, yet lived in a state of bliss. It is said that he "had a strange faculty about him, witnessed very often, of changing carnivorous persons into vegetarians, a mere glance from him seemed enough to destroy the desire for animal food."[41]

Charles Fillmore, who with Myrtle Fillmore founded the Unity movement, said that as people develop spiritually, they naturally begin to develop a desire to stop eating meat. "There is a kindred spirit in all living things—a love for life," says Charles, "Any man who considers honestly the oneness of life feels an aversion to eating meat."[42]

AN INVOCATION

Let me intreat thee, O . . . reader,
by all that is good and kind and just;
Let me intreat thee for God's sake,
for Christ's sake, for man's sake,
for the sake of the animals—
Yea, and for thine own sake.

Make it your business, esteem it your duty,
believe it to be the ground of your hope
and know that it is that which the Lord doth
require of thee: "to do justly, to love mercy
and to walk humbly with thy God."

*See that no animal of any kind, whether
entrusted to thy care, or coming across
thy path, suffer through thy neglect or abuse.*

*Let no hope of profit,
no compliance with custom,
and no fear of the ridicule of the world,
ever tempt thee to the least act of cruelty
or injustice to any creature whatsoever.
Blessed are the merciful,
for they shall obtain mercy.*
—Reverend Humphrey Primatt, d. 1790[43]

Chapter Six

THE TRANSFORMING POWER OF POSITIVE THOUGHT AND PRAYER

Most men consider the course of events as natural and inevitable. They little know what radical changes are possible through prayer.
—Paramahansa Yogananda[1]

How Prayer Can Help the Animals
Prayer or positive thought is an essential ingredient in all our efforts for the animals, for the earth, for world

peace, and for our own inner peace. Whether our focus is legislation, vigils, demonstrations, education, rescue work, or other service, positive thought adds energy, faith, momentum, and fire to the work. But this is not its only function. A far more important purpose of positive thought is that it deals directly with the deep and ultimate cause of the world's ills. That cause is the fear that drives humanity's greed and lust for power. Prayer, positive thought, and spiritual vision take direct aim at that fear. They have the power, scientifically applied and coupled with action, to change the world.

Subversive Prayer for the Highest Good

Rabbi Abraham Joshua Heschel tells us that prayer means nothing "unless it is subversive." He says prayer must have as its aim "to overthrow and to ruin the pyramids of callousness, hatred, opportunism, and falsehood." He challenges the liturgical movement to become revolutionary and to "overthrow the forces that continue to destroy the promise, the hope, the vision."[2]

Our world, as it is now, is a product of all our thoughts. As this fact becomes more widely known around the world, increasing numbers of people are joining in global prayer efforts for peace on earth. Worldwide peace prayers are being shared on many Web sites, including:

www.emissaryoflight.com
www.greggbraden.com

www.worldpuja.org
www.yogananda-srf.org
and my Web site at www.premarinfree.com.

These efforts and many others all around the world
intend to save the earth from oblivion by holding the
clear vision that we are transcending from our present
fear-based mindset to a global heartset that knows no
fear, that knows only love.

Most of the global prayers are focused on peace for
humanity. A few add a word or two about "all life" or
"the earth." These projects are dedicated to the historic
vision of true world peace. As voices for the voiceless,
we can join this enormous wave of prayer energy that
is transforming the planet. We can add our specific
prayers and visions for peace and compassion for the
animals. And we can ask our brothers and sisters who
are visualizing world peace for people to join us as we
join them. Together our prayer power will be truly
subversive.

Our thoughts are not confined or limited to our
physical brains. When we pray, our prayers do not rat-
tle around inside our heads. They operate outside the
boundaries of space, time, and our bodies. They become
part of the infinite Love that is present for all. The new
paradigm with regard to prayer and thought is, as
Wayne Dyer named his book, "You'll see it when you
believe it."[3] Spiritual teachers have known this for cen-

turies. Now their wisdom is becoming our wisdom. First we know it and believe it. Then it manifests and we see it. Jesus said, "Everything you ask in prayer, *believing*, you shall receive." (Matthew 21: 22).

We are little creators given free will to fashion the world we want. But we have created a ferocious world full of greed, hate, and destruction. All our fears have come upon us. We have literally manifested the world we fear, unaware that we had such power. I see a time coming soon when *all our love will come upon us*. We can and will consciously, intentionally, deliberately create a compassionate world for the animals and for us.

The United Church of Religious Science, Christian Scientists, and others pray for healing in a way quite consistent with the ancient teachings and the principles of physics. The key is to see only perfection and to know there is nothing that needs healing, only something that needs revealing. Belief in the power of the Divine Spirit is more powerful than the belief that undesirable conditions are necessary.[4]

Gandhi's belief in the power of prayer was absolutely granite-solid. He called prayer an act more real than acts of eating or drinking. "It is no exaggeration to say that they [prayer, worship, and supplication] alone are real, all else is unreal."[5] Without prayer, said Gandhi, "there is no inward peace."[6]

Paramahansa Yogananda, a twentieth-century spiritual teacher, likens our minds to radios. When we free our minds from distractions, which he says are like static to a radio, we can send out powerful thoughts and waves of love.

Imagine the impact millions of us would have if we tuned our radios to God energy and sent clear images and prayers of beauty, serenity, and love to all the animals and people of earth. As fears dissipate and tensions subside, love comes rushing in. When authentic love rushes in, a sense of connectedness to all life comes trailing in behind it like long tail feathers. It may be tenuous at first, but if we keep sending and the collective unconscious keeps receiving, we will be astounded at the results.

How many of us light bearers are there? Some say all it takes to ease humanity up a notch in vibrational consciousness is one tenth of one percent. We may have already reached that critical mass. We are lightning unleashed. Let the rains of peace thoughts bring the Garden back to life.

The land that was laid waste has become like the Garden of Eden.—Ezekiel 36: 33–35

Leaping Consciousness: "The Hundredth Monkey"
The "Hundredth Monkey" story relates the phenomenon of how consciousness can leap from one group to another. Monkeys on the island of Koshima began washing the sand off of sweet potatoes given to them by

observing scientists. This was a new behavior with pleasant consequences. More and more monkeys learned to wash their potatoes in this way until suddenly, as if a thought form had taken wings and flown across the sea, monkeys on other islands, and the monkeys on the mainland at Takasakiyama, began to spontaneously wash their sweet potatoes as well.[7]

New ideas gather density and power as more beings become aware of them. We certainly witness this in the world of technology. Many discoveries have been made simultaneously in different parts of the world, and technological knowledge is growing exponentially as never before. Over the centuries people have been praying in various ways for "heaven" to come to earth. We are standing now, each on our respective islands, washing the sand off of our ancient visions and cleansing them in the purifying streams. We are tasting the possibility of heaven on earth, seeing it, feeling it, and believing it.

As we do this, the lower vibration of a competitive world full of fear begins to fade and receive less emotion and attention. We, in turn, experience a higher vibration as individuals and a greater harmony with the Divine Energy of the Universe. This is what Thoreau was talking about when he said that we can pass through an invisible barrier, after which "new, universal, and more liberal laws will begin to establish themselves" within us, and we "will live with the license of a higher order of beings."

The Science of Prayer

Over 200 scientific studies have documented a connection between longevity and spiritual faith. People with faith have less depression, less addiction, and better health outcomes with regard to cancer, high blood pressure, and heart disease. Prayer and meditation stimulate relaxation and lower blood pressure, heart and breathing rates.[8]

And here's a fascinatingly synchronistic finding. Scientific studies also show that being in the presence of a loving companion animal also lowers blood pressure, heart and breathing rates. What is the healing, soothing factor? Both with animals and with prayer, we are in the presence of pure unconditional Love.

Not only does prayer help the person who is praying, but science is also validating the ageless wisdom that praying for others has beneficial effects as well.[9] Polls taken by *Time*/CNN and *USA Weekend* revealed that "about 80 percent of Americans believe spiritual faith or prayer can help people recover from illness or injury."[10]

Some may say that praying for one's brother who has high blood pressure may seem a bit insignificant compared to praying for the violence that is affecting the earth. But all prayer helps. The animals and the earth can wait no longer. I wrote this book because I believe so much that, with enough of us holding the positive vision of compassion for all, we can raise the vibration of earth and create love wherever it is needed.

High blood pressure and heart rate are physical reactions to fear. Prayers send love. Love lowers both, because "perfect Love casts out fear." The blood pressure of the human race is soaring and the heart of humankind is racing from all the fear thoughts. If enough of us send Love, we will witness a miracle that will leave us in eternal awe.

Gregg Braden recently released his new book *The Isaiah Effect: Decoding the Lost Science of Prayer and Prophecy*. He believes that the science of effective prayer has been "encrypted in ancient traditions" for centuries, and we are now finally becoming able to fully understand it. With a sufficient union of thought, feeling, and emotion, scientific prayer can be used to bring desired changes into the physical world. Many ancient prophecies foretell of Armageddon and global catastrophes, but Braden points out that prophecies are not claiming inevitable outcomes. Instead, they let us know that we can choose our future. Collectively, we can work a miracle.[11]

We attract what we fear.
We attract what we love.
Should we not choose love?

Churches and Prayer

The power of prayer was discovered eons ago by a few wise people. A few scientists are now lending their voices in support of the validity of prayer. Even a few medical schools are offering courses in religion, faith, and spirituality.

Some religions are teetering back and forth on their views on the power of prayer, but the majority do actively encourage their members to pray for human problems to be resolved. What seems to be sadly missing is any widespread emphasis among religions to pray for and actively help the animals and the earth.

Joel Kurz, a pastor of a Lutheran parish in Pennsylvania, decries the neglect of nature by the Christian churches. "If we were to collectively rid this world of the lilies of the field, could we still ponder the full splendor of the divine?"[12]

Andrew Linzey, an Anglican priest who holds the world's first post in theology and animal welfare, has written a book entitled *Animal Rites: Liturgies of Animal Care.* This most unusual book is a collection of liturgies written specifically for animals and designed to be read by a priest and his or her congregation. The liturgies are written for animal funerals, memorials, adoptions, healing, protection, and many other wonderful prayers. I highly recommend this book for Christian churches everywhere.

Reverend Linzey has written this book to fill what he feels is a void in Christian churches. "Almost nowhere," he says, "in the common prayers and liturgies of the Christian church—for almost two millen-

nia—do we find prayers for God's non-human creatures.
. . . [I]t is as though the world of animals was simply
invisible."[13]

Fifteen hundred years ago, Saint Isaac the Syrian
explained that if one is truly compassionate, then one's
heart has no boundaries. It embraces all creation, not
just people. It is the boundless heart, full of compassion,
that fuels prayer with ultimate power. He said:

> *It is a heart which is burning with love for the
> whole creation, for [humans], for the birds, for
> the beasts, for the demons—for all creatures.
> [Someone] who has such a heart cannot see or
> call to mind a creature without [their] eyes
> being filled with tears by reason of the immense
> compassion which seizes [their] heart; a heart
> which is softened and can no longer bear to see
> or learn from others of any suffering, even the
> smallest pain, being inflicted on a creature . . .
> That is why such a [person] never ceases to pray
> also for the animals . . .*[14]

Saint Isaac was among the few who spoke out for
the voiceless in those times. Today, however, we have
respected theologians such as Linzey, Matthew Fox, and
others making credible and important the act of praying
for the animals. Change is in the air.

Nevertheless, we cannot wait for the churches to make praying for animals a mainstream tradition. We can and must pray for the animals on our own. And we can pray for the churches and temples that have not yet awakened to the great power they have to bring healing and peace to the animal nations. All change begins with thought, and prayer is thought. It has been said that "with prayer we create without hands." The key to life taught by all religions is this: Love one another. Although this has historically been misinterpreted by most to mean love only human beings, shamans and mystics and we ourselves know that we are to love all beings, not just humans. This is the key to peace on earth and a joyful life.

The God of all is Love for all Creation. God's energy is constantly moving in the direction of humans and all beings freely *choosing Love, thinking Love, and acting in Love.* Our hearts are moving us to become the compassion and peace we seek for the animals and the earth.

TOGETHER WE CAN DO THIS
By
CHOOSING
THINKING
PRAYING
ACTING
AND BEING LOVE.

Chapter Seven

PRAYER POWER IN ACTION

Praying and visualizing are very personal actions. I am not going to tell anyone *how* to pray. What feels right to you may not work for me and vice versa. Prayers or positive thought can be as complicated as a day-long ritual or as simple as talking to God on the way to work. But there are special qualities of prayer that empower the person that is praying as well as the prayers and thoughts themselves. These qualities are:

> Joy, Gratitude, and Devotion
> Positive Vision and Will Power
> Forgiveness
> Trust, Faith, and Surrender

Joy, Gratitude, and Devotion

One day, St. Francis was walking about rejoicing in God's love. Along the way, he saw an almond tree. "Brother Almond, speak to me of God," he called out. Immediately, the almond tree burst into full bloom.

More joyful than ever, St. Francis continued on to a little pool of water beside a creek. "Brother Creek," he sang, "speak to me of God." Answering bubbles appeared in the quiet water and then, as Francis gazed into the pool, the water became mirror-like. In it St. Francis saw the face of his spiritual sister Clare.

His joy was overflowing as he approached a tree full of birds. "Little birds, my brothers, speak to me of God," he said. With that the birds sang together a melody he had never heard before. Then they flew up into the air, forming a cross in the sky.

Shortly, he came upon a pilgrim carrying a pack on his back. St. Francis made the same request of the pilgrim. Silently the pilgrim took the saint's hand and together they went into the city to the poorest area. There they sat on a bench and began distributing bread to the hungry people.

As the bread was shared, it multiplied until all were full. The pilgrim then looked toward heaven and said first, "Our Father," then, "Our bread." Francis's joy knew no bounds, for that day he witnessed God in all things.[1] Joy is an emotion powerful enough to move mountains. Prayers and thoughts infused with the magnetism of joy pull in results. Ecstasy is born in gratitude for the tiniest blade of grass and the air we breathe.

Paramahansa Yogananda says that prayer filled with devotion is the most effective prayer, because "Devotion, love for God, is the magnetic attraction of the heart that God cannot resist." If one calls out, "O Lord, I love You!' [then] into that devotee's heart He comes running."[2]

Positive Vision and Will Power

I heard a song on the radio once about a little boy who wanted to be a baseball player, and in the song he practices diligently all by himself. He pitches the ball up in the air for himself, swings his bat and misses. He pitches again. Up in the air goes the ball. Down it comes. He swings and misses again. Again and again he tries. Each time he fails to connect with the ball. Finally, his mother calls him home to dinner. As he strides along toward home, he thinks to himself, "I must be the best pitcher that ever lived." Now that's positive thinking. Even if he doesn't become a great ball player, that young man will succeed at life.

We can create a positive future by "creating positive images of the future that, magnet-like, pull us in the direction we desire."[3] Yogananda tells us, from many years of experience, "When you persist, refusing to accept failure, the object of will must materialize. . . . Even though there is nothing in the world to conform to your wish, when your will persists, the desired result will somehow manifest."[4] Although there is little in the world that conforms to our vision for compassion for all the animals, nevertheless if we persist and never give up, such will be the essence of the new heaven on earth.

Forgiveness and Humility

And whenever you stand praying, forgive if you have anything against anyone . . .

—Jesus in Mark 11:25

What did Jesus mean when he said, "Father forgive them; for they do not know what they are doing" (Luke 23:34)? They certainly knew they were killing Jesus. What they did not know, however, went much deeper than that.

- They didn't know that Jesus was their brother, that they were intimately connected to him and that by killing him they were killing a part of themselves.
- They didn't know that they were acting out of fear toward Jesus. They thought they were acting out of power and righteousness. Acting in fear does not solve problems but only creates new ones.
- They didn't know they could act out of love toward Jesus and that acting solely from a place of love would bring about the highest and best results.
- They didn't know that the political and economic power they sought was a drug that promised happiness but rarely delivered it; a drug that, in fact, would continue to drive them to more violence in relentless attempts to maintain their power.
- They didn't know that they already had all they needed within them to achieve joy, love, and a life without fear. They did not know that no

one, not even Jesus, could take their inner peace away from them.

- They didn't know how to truly empower themselves. They hadn't yet learned that true power comes only when one learns how to love all creation unconditionally.

- They didn't know that death is not real—that they and Jesus and all other beings are eternal spirits living forever as one Divine family.

- They didn't know that we are all divine spirits who are here for one simple reason: to learn to be embodiments of love here on earth.

All over the world, there are people committing unspeakable acts of violence against people, animals, trees, plants, and the earth. Why are they doing this? It is because they don't know what they are doing. Just as those who crucified Jesus didn't know all the truths listed above, the people actively engaged in animal cruelty today are equally ignorant.

- They do not yet understand that the animals and others that they are hurting and killing are their brothers and sisters and that by hurting them they are hurting themselves. The vibrations caused by the violence reverberate throughout the world and boomerang back to the senders every time.

- They do not yet understand that they are acting out of fear and a sense that without such violence they cannot live.
- They do not yet know that if they frame their actions with love and compassion they will get the best results.
- They do not yet know that economic, scientific, or political power gained through violence can never be satisfying. Instead, power gained in this way increases the fear of losing that power and leads to the escalation of violence.
- They do not yet know that all the power and peace and love that they need is within them and does not need to be acquired outside of themselves, nor can anyone take that power, peace, and love away from them unless they let them.
- They do not yet know that the only real way to gain personal power, love, and inner peace is by learning to love all creation unconditionally.
- They do not yet understand that all creation, including themselves, is sacred, divine, and eternal. Indeed, God knows every sparrow that falls.
- They do not yet understand that we are all spiritual beings come to earth for one reason: to learn to express our true nature as miraculous embodiments of love.

Gandhi was once stranded on a ship with his family and many other Indians in the port of Durban, South Africa. The white residents of Durban were threatening to push them into the sea if they did not return to India. While on board, Gandhi was asked how he would remain true to his principle of nonviolence if the whites carried out their threats. Gandhi replied, "I hope God will give me the courage and the sense to forgive them and to refrain from bringing them to law. I have no anger against them. I am only sorry for their ignorance and their narrowness. I know that they sincerely believe that what they are doing today is right and proper. I have no reason therefore to be angry with them."[5]

As we seek to awaken ourselves, we help all others to awaken as well and to know the truth of who we all are and why we are here. We can communicate to them, without anger or fear, that all life is sacred, and that they too are sacred beings. If we know people engaged in cruelty, we can talk to them, and as Jane Goodall says in her book *Reason for Hope*, we can "try to reach gently into their hearts."

Many workers in labs and slaughterhouses and other places of torture and death have witnessed the forgiveness in the eyes of their innocent victims. Each time an innocent is killed, there is forgiveness, and there is potential for the resurrection of mercy in the hearts of the workers. Also, each one who has been oppressed or tortured or killed has an immortal spirit that lives on and is loved no matter what violence has been done to the body. All spiritual teachers agree: we never die. Life itself cannot die. From that point of view, we can see that those who are suffering the most are not the animals, but rather their torturers and murderers, for it is they who have temporarily lost touch with their own souls, just as we all do when we commit violence.

In truth, there is nothing for us to forgive, only anger to release from our hearts. True humility, the state of being what Gandhi and St. Francis called being "a zero," is the realization that we are not separate from anyone or the judge of anyone. As Martin Luther King said, it is the action that is harmful, not the people.

We can bring more love into the world. That is the ultimate resurrection, the ultimate meaning of Jesus' life. Out of all the death, destruction, wars, and suffering, we can resurrect love over and over again, until finally there will be so much transfigured love lighting up the earth that fear and suffering will no longer be able to grow in the fertile fields of compassion and wisdom.

Trust, Faith, and Surrender

Imagine you are a dog tied to a tree. You don't like it at all, and you want to get free. But the more you run and pull and yank, the more you wind yourself around the tree. The rope around your neck gets shorter and tighter. Suddenly, from out of nowhere, a human appears. She sits down nearby and tells you she will untie you, but you have to hold still and trust her so she can get to the rope. If you keep running and jumping and barking, she can't get close enough to let you loose. Now imagine the tension within you as you decide to stop, in spite of your fear, and simply trust her to set you free. It is a difficult decision to surrender and trust. James Twyman used this little metaphor at a peace conference to create a deeper understanding of trust and surrender.

One of the greatest healing discoveries of all time is the Twelve Step Program, originally used by Alcoholics Anonymous and now used in many groups recovering from other challenges. The third step of the twelve steps is this: "We made a decision to turn our will and our lives over to the care of God as we understood Him."[6] Implicit in this step is the understanding that we cannot break our addictions without help. Just as we cannot break our own personal addictions alone, humanity cannot break its addiction to animal cruelty alone. We need the help of the Great Spirit.

It is the divine power of love that holds atoms together and exists in every tiny pebble and in every majestic mountain and in every one of us. And we can't create this world of peace and beauty without surrendering to the Will of Love. We will each find our own ways of doing that and of making our peace with our Higher Power. We will each find a way to trust that Love has the highest wisdom, that it can unchain us from our frustrations and fears and lead us into the spiritual freedom that we need to help the animals. I trust that we all can and will.

When Jesus says "Believe that you have received," he means "Let it go." Know that your prayer is answered. Don't worry and stew, because worrying magnetizes the situation right back into existence.

Part of this process involves a certain amount of emotional release from the problems we are trying to solve. It is essential that we develop this release, because of the simple law that like attracts like. When we are full of anger and hatred, we add those vibrations to the world and actually create more of what we are working to end and attract it to ourselves. Ram Dass said, "[W]hen you see any kind of injustice in the world, if you are attached to it being any other way, you are at one level perpetuating the polarization even as you are working to end it."[7] The detachment to which he refers is not indifference. It is a release which bears witness to the healing that is needed and then releases it to its true perfection.

> *When you embrace uncertainty and include intention and detachment, then the most improbable happens. That's what we call a miracle.*—Deepak Chopra[8]

Three Types of Prayers

The Hindu teacher Shankara describes three kinds of prayer. The first is dualism. In dualism, God is separate from us, a being or energy that can help us if we communicate our needs. The Lord's Prayer is a dualistic prayer, because we address our Father who is in Heaven.

The second is qualified non-dualism. In this realm of understanding, we sense our relationship to the Divine. We are the children made of the same substance as the divine parent; or we are the branches of the divine tree. So when we pray, we sense that the same power that is in God is also in us.

Fully non-dualistic prayer is really beyond prayer, because when we reach the state of non-dualism we are not communicating to an "other." We are the prayer itself.

We all travel back and forth along this continuum. Sometimes I see my hands reaching out to God above in desperate supplication. At other times, more centered times, I look at my hands in wonder and I say, "Oh God, these are Your hands. Do with them as you will." And then there are those rare, non-dual moments of bliss in which my hands are everywhere and nowhere, embracing all.

Jesus is very real to me. I feel his presence with me all the time. My prayers with Jesus are really conversations. He is my teacher and healer and friend, separate from me in identity, yet somehow working through me, and always comforting me from deep within. When I meditate, he helps me feel my oneness and understand that there is no duality. Some gurus live in that non-dual state. Most of us only visit it now and then. But our prayers are powerful nonetheless.

As long as our passionate intentions are fixed on love alone, our style of praying does not matter. It is said that "a short prayer pierces the heavens." If we simply cry out, "God help the animals!" and mean it with all our hearts, our prayer will be heard.

A Scientific, Affirmative Prayer Formula That Works

Because of the law of attraction, the power of passionate intention, and the divinity that lives and breathes in each one of us, the following prayer formula is power-packed. Here are the steps:

1. Acknowledge the problem or challenge.
2. Know that the problem has no real power. Only Love has power.
3. Pray and affirm that the best and most loving outcome already exists and is ready to take form.
4. Imagine that outcome; use all your senses to feel it as reality. Breathe power into it.
5. Feel your oneness with the universe, with the Divine, and with the answered prayer and the beings involved.
6. Release it with joy to the nurturing care of God. And so it is. And all is well.

We bear witness to the violence and the cruelty.
We acknowledge the suffering of the innocents
and the perpetrators, including ourselves.
And then, from the depths and heights of Truth itself,
We deny violence and cruelty any power.
Their shadows fade to nothing in the Light of Love.

PART TWO

THE PRAYERS
*Blessings, Prayers, Vows, and Visions
for the Animals and for Peace*

Part Two

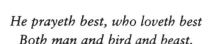

He prayeth best, who loveth best
Both man and bird and beast,

He prayeth best, who loveth best
All things both great and small;
For the dear God who loveth us,
He made and loveth all.*
—Samuel Taylor Coleridge (1772–1834)

The second section of this book contains positive thoughts, prayers, blessings, affirmations, vows, pledges, and visualizations. Some were written or spoken many years ago, some I have written, and some come from our contemporaries. There are prayer lists that list various entities in different categories that need our light and good vibrations. There are also prayers and meditations for specific animal nations, and thoughts and prayers for specific situations that call upon us to keep our spirits centered on the Light.

My goal in assembling this collection is to help us settle into a peaceful, prayerful frame of mind and to become deliverers of Divine healing energy to the suffering animals of the world. In doing so we:

- Form a conscious partnership with the Creator expressing our willingness to bring Heaven to earth and to bring Divine Love into its full flowering on earth.
- Hold a vision together of a world encircled with Radiant Compassion for all beings; a world of true peace and universal harmony.
- Communicate spirit to spirit with all the animals of earth, indeed all beings of earth, that this vision we hold is the true reality of who we all really are, the truth that has been so long hidden behind the shadows of violence and fear. And communicate spirit-to-spirit that we need to allow the Loving Hand of God to awaken us to our true inner nature.

---

*These lines are from the famous poem "The Rime of the Ancient Mariner." The main message of the poem is that we will suffer in life until we understand in our hearts that all creatures are worthy of love, care, and reverence. Spiritual growth cannot go forward without this realization. The poem caused a rise in consciousness in England in the 1800s. The Royal Society for the Prevention of Cruelty to Animals was founded at that time, and vegetarianism gained in popularity partly as a result of Coleridge's epic poem.[1]

We are all beloved children of the same devoted Creator, journeying together into our own perfection, which already exists in us, because we are made of God-stuff.

There is no magical formula for prayer here in these pages. The magic is in you, in your loving heart. The more often these prayers are read or spoken and the more people who make use of them the more power for good they will radiate. There is also immense love-force in simply holding the book to your heart or placing your hand on it while meditating. Such acts focus your attention, if even for a moment, on the creation of more love for all beings. Such acts literally and absolutely create more love.

Chapter Eight

GENERAL PRAYERS FOR THE ANIMALS

Prayer of St. Francis of Assisi
(with some additions I think he would like)

LORD,
Make me an instrument of your peace.

Where there is hatred
    for animal rights activists,
    for hunters and trappers,
    for vivisectionists and corporate polluters,
    for snakes and spiders,
    for weeds and weather,
    for any being anywhere,
Let me sow Love
    for me and everyone.

Where there is injury
    to animals in laboratories, slaughterhouses,
      factory farms, zoos, circuses, rodeos, fur

farms, rivers, oceans, forests, and plains;
to animal liberationists;
to all people who work at jobs where
    animals are harmed or killed;
to trees and plants and all beings everywhere,
Let me sow pardon and healing
    for me and everyone.

Where there is doubt
    that the violence of humans toward each other
    and toward animals and their ecosystems will
    ever end,
Let me sow faith
    in me and everyone.

Where there is despair
    because of our long history of war,
    selfishness, greed, fear, and ignorance,
Let me sow hope
    that we are evolving into a new creature with
    the elevated consciousness of compassion and
    reverence for all life.

Where there is darkness
    in all the hidden places:
    laboratories, slaughterhouses,
    factory farms, violent homes,
    in the pet trade and the bushmeat trade

and in our own hearts
Let me shine the light of transformation.

And where there is sadness
among animal, peace, and environmental
advocates,
among the many animals in cages,
among the animals separated from their
families,
among those starving for affection or food,
Let me sow joy
in myself and all beings everywhere.

Oh, Divine Master,
Grant that I may not so much seek
To be consoled, as to console,
To be understood, as to understand,
To be loved, as to love.
For it is in the giving that we receive.
It is in the pardoning that we are pardoned,
And it is in the dying that we are born
to eternal life.
Amen.

The Prayer of the Prodigal Children
Mother-Father God, Divine Spirit of Love,
We know you understand that we are in the
adolescence of our development in consciousness.

We are the prodigal sons and daughters who have taken the riches of this heavenly earth, and in our youthful ignorance and fear we have used up those riches instead of caring for them.

Help us to come back home to You, where we know You will hold out Your loving arms in welcome and fall at our feet in pure joy that we have awakened to who we really are and returned to where we belong.

Help us to awaken together and quickly that we may set about our tasks as Your adult children repairing the damage we've done, cleaning and healing the earth, freeing and healing our little brother and sister animals, and finally, after all these years, aligning our wills with yours to create on earth, as it is in Heaven.

Mitakuye Oyas'in,* Amen, Thank You, God.

A Prayer to Be Awakened
Dear Lord of Love,
Stand by me and wake me
Refuse to let me sleep and tell me again
That I asked you to wake me.
And that I asked you to create in me
A smooth and open pathway for You to move

---

*Mitakuye Oyas'in is a Native American Lakota phrase that means "all my relations." It is spoken reverently in ceremonies to honor all animals and all of creation.

through all my cells,
through every breath I take,
through every thought I think,
through every beat of my heart.
Work through me to bring Your peace
to all precious beings everywhere.
Thank You, God.

A Short Blessing for the Animals
May all my sacred
brothers and sisters
Walk,
Fly,
Swim, and
Move
In Love, Peace, and Freedom.

A Prayer to Help Us Hold the Vision
Heavenly Creator,
You whose magnetic love
has kept us ever seeking you,
Help us to keep our vision close and real
in our hearts and minds and souls.
Help us project it out on rays of light
beaming from our hearts.

Help us to hold
this grand vision of all of us

finally transcending into our true nature
as beings of universal, transcendent love.
We see this magnificent earth populated
by kind humans who are fearless
because You are in each one of us.
And in this fearlessness we find no need
for violence of any kind toward anyone.
We live in harmony and mutual respect
with all animals and all creation.
Only Divine kindness and compassion,
love and light express through us
as we stand all rapt in awe
at the holy wonder of the loving universe.
Om, Shanti, Shanti.

**A Prayer of Thanksgiving for the Sacredness of
Life and the Courage to Work for the Animals**
Divine God and Goddess,
We are here loving You, breathing in the
air of earth and the pure Light of the Holy One.
Always we are immersed in the Divine Stream,
But Ah! to stop and really feel the cleansing
spray of it, cool and pure!

We open our hearts wide to You, Creator of
all that is, that lives in us
and lives in all beings,
Bless us and help us to see what we need to see

And help us to feel Your unfathomable
Love for all life
more deeply than ever before.

We are learning that all matter and all the
created world is SACRED, and so we are sacred.
We are learning that each one of us is a
unique union of matter and spirit,
of heaven and earth, of spirit and soul.
Help us as we co-create with You
this sacred soul of ours.

Thank you for cradling us, for carrying us,
for walking with us, for healing and loving us,
for never leaving us, for filling us with
Your mysterious, miraculous light.

Thank You for giving us this clear and passionate
love for the animals and for giving us the boldness
to pray,
to work,
to teach, and
to take action
for their liberation.
Om, Amen.

A Prayer to *Be* Compassion
I understand that
To find compassion for animals,

I must *be* compassion.
To obtain peace for the animals, I must *be* peace.
To gain love for the animals, I must *be* love.

Help me, Dear Lord of Compassion, to *be*
in heart, soul, body, word, and deed
that which I want to manifest
on earth for the animals
and for us all.
Thank You, God.

An Irish Blessing for the Animals
May the earth rise to meet you;
May the wind be always at your back;
May the sun shine warm upon your face,
The rain fall soft upon your lands,
Until we meet again,
May God hold you
in the hollow of Her hand.

**A Short Prayer of Joy and Thanks to See God
in Everything**
Dearest Lord of Love,
I see You
in all of me and all that is.
My heart is won by Your Wonder.
We are all so One-derful
in our Oneness with You.
Thank You, God.

A Prayer for Comfort for the Animals

Oh, dance for the animals, dear Lord of Love,
Caress them as You caress me,
For they tremble alone in cages so small
With no hope to ever be free.

My heart breaks each day, for their pain is mine,
But You strengthen my heart
With Your promise sublime
That one day a great cry of anguish will tear
Through the veil of cruelty now everywhere.
And people from all walks of life will wake up.
We will sob and cry to see what we have done
To the voiceless, the helpless, the gentle and meek,
With grief in our throats and unable to speak,

Then, finally, a vow will come out from all hearts,
Through tears and hearts broken,
A vow of no harm.
A vow of ahimsa*: No harm shall we do
To any being, no matter who.
A heaven we're making right here on earth.
Right now, forever, to Love we give birth.
So dance for the animals, dear Lord of Love,
Caress them as You caress me,
And whisper softly to each one of them,
We will work until they're all free.

---

*Ahimsa: The Hindu vow of nonviolence and compassion for all
beings. See Chapter Five.

A Short Affirmation for Daily Use
The highest good and universal compassion
prevails for all the animals of earth.

A Prayer of Joy for God in Everything
Blessed am I and every being.
All is light and love.
We are awakening to who we are.
We are yawning and stretching.
Take our hands, Oh Lord who is
within us and all around us.
Dance with us in circles until we cannot see
Where You end and we begin.
Whirling 'round and 'round.
You are The Lover, My Lover.
You love only me, and I am everyone,
And I am You.

How can You come dance with me?
You walk toward me in my lover.
You walk beside me in my child.
You peer out from the woods at me in the wolf.
Your hand is tiny.
Your hand is bigger than the earth,
And You touch my lashes
With Your delicate fingers.
And You cradle the earth in Your palm.
And I am a riverbed,

And You are the river flowing in me.
And all my life I've longed for You,
While You followed me like a star,
Shining down upon the manger of my soul.
A million holy nights have passed
While You waited for me to see.

Touch me again, Oh Lord,
Awaken me with Your kiss.
I have slept so long without You,
And I do adore You so.
How can I move from this place at your feet?
Gazing only at You, rapt in awe and wonder
Transfixed with joy.
Teach me, sweet Lord,
To see Your feet Everywhere!

**A Joyful Prayer about Our Oneness with
God and Nature**
I do feel my God
Always with me
Behind my shoulder,
Blowing wisps of my hair.

Yet I must say
That as I sit,
Breathing in this river,
The Divine breaks into me.

Shattering all distraction,
Drawing me to one point of focus,
And the river flows from my eyes.

Ecstasy flows before me
Over rounded stones and jumping fish,
And that same exuberant joy
Draws down into me.
I am mirrored in the dance of Light.
I am One with the River that is God,
that is fish and stones and me.
One, One, One . . .

"I Am An Instrument" Affirmation

I am an instrument of peace.
I am a lighthouse of love.
Today I go with God in me
To spread peace, light, and love
With all my thoughts, words, and deeds.

Transformative Prayer for Institutions of Cruelty: Laboratories, Slaughterhouses, Factory Farms, and Others

Dear Lord of Heaven and Earth and all that is,
You who are the energy of
whole and perfect love and light,
Move through me now
as I focus my love and light

and as I focus the love and light that flow
through me from You in an endless stream.
Make me a beacon of your Love-light
and shine through me now.
I now focus this radiance
and this Divine transforming Love
on all animal laboratories,
all factory farms and slaughterhouses,
all fur farms, circuses, zoos,
marine parks, rodeos, whaling ships,
pesticide and other chemical manufacturers,
fishing, hunting and trapping organizations,
and all other institutions
that cause the suffering of innocent beings.
I can see the cosmic rays
of Your everlasting Love
pouring down upon these places.
Within this light, there can be
no fear
no hatred
no ignorance
no greed.
Within this light, there can be
only YOUR LOVE.

And as these institutions are infused and blessed
by the light of your Love
I see those who work there being transformed,

as they open their eyes to see the glorious
beauty and sacredness in the animals there.
I see their hearts opening, finding the inner peace
that comes through loving kindness to all creation.
And as these institutions are bathed and blessed
by the light of your undying Love for all creation,
I see the animals feeling Your peace, Your comfort
as You embrace each one of them
and bless their spirits.

Help us, Father-Mother God,
to grow bolder and more fearless every day
and guide us closely and clearly
as we work and pray
to end the suffering of the innocents
and bring Your Heaven to earth.
And so it is.
Thank You, God.

Personal Affirmation of Empowerment
I am a bright star shining for God,
A divine child filled with awe and wonder
at who I am, at who we all are.
I am born anew today totally aware
of my own radiance, my courage,
my boldness, and my infinite ability
to give and receive love.
I am an emissary of light.

I go forth today to be love,
to be peace, and to be compassion
for the animals, and for all that is.

Listening in the Silence
Gentle Spirit,
I still my body and my mind.
I relax completely and surrender myself
to You within me.
I send peace to all beings
and listen to You in the silence.

Calling the Animals to Share Our Vision
for a Compassionate World
To all dolphins, elephants, seals, whales, spiders,
all my brothers and sisters of the animal nations,
We are always connected by our kinship
and our mutual divinity.
I am now consciously connecting with you
from my mind to yours, from my heart to yours.
Together, let us hold the vision
of a world filled with love,
where humans no longer attack you,
kill you, imprison you, torture you, or enslave you.
A world in which we all communicate
from one species to another,
just as the races of humans are doing now.
A world in which all species understand

the sacredness of all life
and the oneness and interconnectedness we share.
A vision of us all waking up to who we are
as we evolve the entire creation
toward our destiny as spirits
manifesting beauty, truth, universal love,
and freedom in physical form.

As I reach out to all of you, my heart aches
for the suffering that you continue to endure
at the hands of human beings
all over the earth and sea.
May you find hope and comfort in knowing that
there are millions of us now who are working
to end your suffering and to begin the healing.
There are millions of us working to educate
those who do not yet understand
who you are.
There are millions of us now keeping you
in our hearts and in our prayers.
We know that your spirits join with our spirits
as we hold this vision of a
WORLD ENCIRCLED WITH
LOVE FOR ALL BEINGS
And so it is.
Mitakuye Oyas'in. Thank You, God.

**Knowing the Truth That Love Overpowers
Violence and Sets the Animals Free**
I acknowledge the appearance of violence
toward the animals of the world.
And I let go of the misconception that
this violence must continue.
I know with my heart and soul that
violence has no power
when faced with the unlimited power of Love.

I understand that I have the magnetic power
to create, and I choose to do my part
to create a compassionate world.
I know that this universe is filled
with God's limitless abundance
and infinite compassion,
not just for a few, but for all beings.

I open my mind and heart to the vast,
creative resources of the universe
and listen for Divine ideas for the animals.
I give my love and joy along with many others
and I see the animals living healed,
joyful, and free.

Breathe through Me
Breathe through me, Beloved Lord.
Live through me.

Speak through me.
Think through me.
Love through me.
Be through me.

The Animals' Prayer

All life is sacred. All life—not just that of people.
The life of all that appears and does not appear
on earth—all is sacred; all is part of Creator God.
This is our prayer—that you of the human nations
will learn to have reverence for us all. Think upon
the sacredness of everything you touch and see
and walk upon and, yes, the air you breathe.
Allow your heart to fill with love for all life.
Imagine with me the time that is coming when we
will have taught the lions to literally lie down
with the lambs; when you will have taught your
kind to dispense with traps and guns; when people
of all nations will realize their oneness with
each other and all life everywhere;
and heaven will be upon the earth.

Reverence for the life of one species—your own—
is incomplete. It will never lift humanity high
enough for the full expression of God.
Those of you who hear this and understand
my meaning, you are at this very moment lifting
humanity and the global mind to a higher plane.

Yours is a Love born in high places.
Blessings be upon you.
Oh, Great Spirit, bless these words
that they may be heard and understood
all over this sacred earth.
Thank You, God.

Atonement
Oh, Heavenly Creator,
You who forgive all and love all,
help us to make atonement to the animals of earth
for atrocities performed by human beings
against them for centuries.
Link our spirits now with their spirits
so that they may hear our cries
of sorrow and shame
for what we have done to them.

Dear brothers and sisters, we have
tortured you, beaten you, killed, sacrificed,
skinned, sheared, dismembered, and eaten you.
We have scorned you, laughed at your pain,
taken your infants from you, chained you,
caged you, forced you to carry our burdens,
starved you, hooked you, stolen your feathers,
your pleasures, and your sanity.
We have treated you like machines without feelings,
ignoring your screams,

but we were machines without feelings, not you.
You run from our knives, and we chase you
as if we have the right to take the life
that is so dear to you.
We have taken advantage of your loyalty,
even forced you to fight or run to the death
for us, for a few dollars in our pockets.
Century after century, you have given to us
your friendship, fidelity, devotion, hard work,
and you who live in the wild places have
given us glimpses of heaven in your beauty
and looked at us with God's eyes.

All the while, you have been crying out to us
to wake up to our kinship with you.
And we have not heard you.
But now we are awake,
and more are waking with us.
Now we hear you.
We go forward this day,
bearing witness to our atrocities,
bearing witness to your infinite gifts to us,
and honoring your sacred nature.

And here is our gift to you;
here is our atonement,
that we will walk side by side with you,
defending you, teaching people the truth about you,

and working to bring an end
to violence toward animals everywhere.

We call upon the loving universe
and the grace of God
to help us as we humans join with all of you
to affirm the advent of a new day
in which our broken hearts are healed
by your forgiveness,
and your broken hearts are healed
by our awakening to Truth;
and to affirm the dawning
of a new Heaven on Earth
in which atonement
becomes at-one-ment.
Om, Shanti, Shanti.

Affirmations of Truth
I am Infinite Love.
My true Self is God Within,
the source of all Love.
I am generosity and compassion.
I am pure joy and ecstasy.
I am peace walking.

A Christian Prayer for Animal Welfare
Almighty God, we come together to thank you
for the beauty and glory of your creation;

to praise you for your holiness and grace;
to acknowledge our responsibility to animals
and for our use of the created world.
But, first of all, we pray for your forgiveness
because of our part in sins of thoughtlessness
and cruelty towards animal life.

Almighty God, you have given us
temporary lordship of your beautiful creation.
But we have misused our power, turned away
from responsibility and marred your image in us.

Forgive us, true Lord, especially for
our callousness and cruelty to animals.
Help us to follow the way of your Son,
Jesus Christ,
who expressed power in humility
and lordship in loving service.
Enable us, by your Spirit,
to walk in newness of life,
healing injury, avoiding wrong
and making peace with all your creatures.
God of everlasting love, who is eternally forgiving;
pardon and restore us, and make us one with you
in your new creation.
Amen.[2]

A Prayer for the Persecutors of Animals
Lord God,
Your creatures suffer everywhere
at the hands of human beings
afflicted with littleness of heart;
may your blessing be upon them,
and may your Spirit also enlarge
the hearts of their persecutors
that they may repent of their evil
and embrace the way of peace.
Amen.[3]

Global Peace Prayer
I accept peace this moment for myself and for
all sentient beings on this and every planet.
I accept my role as an Emissary of Light,
and I allow this feeling of peace to extend
from me as a blessing to the whole universe.
Peace prevails on earth because the choice has
been made by me, and I join with everyone
around the world who is making the same
choice this very moment.
May Peace Prevail on Earth.
(Repeat the above line three times, then, with
enthusiasm . . .)
Peace Prevails on Earth![4]

The Vision of a Peaceable Kingdom
May the vision of a Peaceable Kingdom
grow in the hearts of all people.
May all creation cry out for justice and shalom,
and may we have ears to hear and hands
to dedicate toward the work of peacemaking.
First Presbyterian Church, IN, 1991

A Prayer for Our Weeping Earth
Our earth weeps for we no longer see divinity
in creation, the sacredness of life. Thus, we
continue to steal fur from the backs of animals;
we continue to steal land from the fox and sparrow
for shopping malls and parking lots.

Thus our earth weeps—Let us pray!

Thunderclouds that once rained pure and clean
are now acidic, killing the trees in the forest,
the fish in the streams.

Thus our earth weeps—Let us pray!

We continue to destroy wetlands and pothole
prairies with our machinery in pursuit of false
dreams and quick profits.

Thus our earth weeps—Let us pray!

In all our plundering we forget that we, too, are a
part of creation in which we destroy. Thus we
must ponder this:
How can we sing when all the songbirds
 have vanished?
How can we breathe when industrial
 fumes suffocate the sky?
How can we feel joy knowing that
 mountain snow no longer supports
 the weight of stalking wolves?
How can we live when our oceans have
 been turned to cesspools by a wasteful society?
How can we know ourselves when
 the great chain of life is broken?
Thus our earth weeps—Let us pray!

To heal our weeping earth we must relearn
to see the beauty of our living planet,
and once again allow our ears to be enchanted
by the song of all songs—life;
and know from the deepest
levels of our soul that we too are
a part of the cosmic unfolding,
so our earth weeps no more.
Let us pray!
Edward Amerson[5]

**St. Basil's Prayer for the Increase
of Human Compassion A.D. 375***
*The earth is the Lord's and the fullness thereof.
Oh, God, enlarge within us the sense of fellowship
with all living things, our brothers the animals
to whom Thou gavest the earth as their home
in common with us.*

*We remember with shame that in the past
we have exercised the high dominion of man
with ruthless cruelty so that the voice of the earth,
which should have gone up to Thee in song,
has been a groan of travail.*

*May we realize that they live not for us alone,
but for themselves and for Thee,
and that they love the sweetness of life.*[6]

An Ancient Hindu Prayer to End Animal Suffering
May all that have life be delivered from suffering.

**Buddhist Prayer for Animals to be
Free from Suffering**
*May all beings be free from enmity;
May all beings be free from injury;
May all beings be free from suffering;
May all beings be happy.*[7]

---

* St. Basil was a theologian and bishop in the early Christian church.
He established the first hospital ever to take care of lepers.

Buddhist Prayer for Peace for All Beings
May all beings everywhere plagued
  with sufferings of body and mind
  quickly be freed from their illnesses.
May those frightened cease to be afraid,
  and may those bound be free.
May the powerless find power,
  and may people think of befriending
  one another.
May those who find themselves in trackless,
  fearful wildernesses—
  the children, the aged, the unprotected—
  be guarded by beneficent celestials,
  and may they swiftly attain Buddhahood.[8]

**Schweitzer's Nighttime Prayer of Protection
and Blessing for the Animals**
Dear God,
Protect and bless all beings that breathe,
keep all evil from them,
and let them sleep in peace.[9]

Hindu Prayer for Friendship with the Animals
O God, scatterer of ignorance and darkness,
grant me your strength.
May all beings regard me with the eye of a friend,
and I all beings! With the eye of a friend
may each single being regard all others.
Sukla Yajur, Veda XXXVI

Jain Prayer for Peace for All Beings

*Peace and Universal Love
is the essence of the Gospel
preached by all the Enlightened Ones.
The Lord has preached that equanimity
is the Dharma.
Forgive do I creatures all,
and let all creatures forgive me.
Unto all have I amity, and unto none enmity.
Know that violence is the root cause of
all the miseries in the world.
Violence, in fact, is the knot of bondage.
"Do not injure any living being."
This is the eternal, perennial,
and unalterable way of spiritual life.
A weapon, howsoever powerful it may be,
can always be superseded by a superior one,
but no weapon can be superior
to nonviolence and love.*[10]

St. Francis's Canticle of the Creatures

*Most High omnipotent good Lord,
To Thee praise, glory, honor, and every blessing.
To Thee alone Most High do they belong.
And no man is worthy to pronounce Thy Name.*

*Praise be to Thee my Lord with all Thy creatures.
Especially for Master Brother Sun*

Who illuminates the day for us,
And Thee Most High he manifests.
Praise be to Thee my Lord for Sister Moon
and for the stars.
In Heaven Thou hast formed them,
shining, precious, fair.

Praise be to Thee my Lord for Brother Wind,
For air and clouds, clear sky, and all the weathers
Through which Thou sustainest all Thy creatures.
Praise be to Thee my Lord for Sister Water
She is useful and humble, precious and pure.

Praise be to Thee my Lord for Brother Fire,
Through him our night Thou dost enlighten,
And he is fair and merry, boisterous and strong.

Praise be to Thee my Lord for our sister
Mother Earth,
Who nourishes and sustains us all,
Bringing forth divers fruits,
and many-colored flowers and herbs.

Praise be to Thee my Lord for those
who pardon grant for love of Thee
And bear infirmity and tribulation,
Blessed be those who live in peace,
For by Thee Most High they shall be crowned.

O bless and praise my Lord all creatures,
And thank and serve Him in deep humility.

Schweitzer's Prayer for Animals Who Are Suffering

Hear our prayer . . .
for the animals that are overworked,
     underfed, and cruelly treated;
for all wistful creatures in captivity
     that beat their wings against bars;
for any that are hunted or lost,
     deserted, frightened, hungry;
for all that are put to death . . .
And for those who deal with them
we ask a heart of compassion
and gentle hands and kindly words.

A Chant to Increase Awareness of Our Oneness with All Life

One with all life, holy I am.

This is generally sung by singing the entire phrase on one note and then going up the musical scale, singing the phrase each time on one note. Or one can simply sing it on one chosen note several times or sing it to a tune. The power of a chant is in the repetition, which helps our minds to leave all other thoughts behind and focus on one truth.

**Three Chants to Say or Sing
to the Animals as Blessings**
All these chants have been set to music. However,
they are powerful whether spoken or sung. A very
wonderful way to use them is to repeat them over
and over, each time thinking of another animal or
group of animals that you wish to bless. For example, when you are repeating the "all I ask of you"
chant, you might first say it to the dog that lives with
you. Then, repeat it again to the Premarin horses,
then the gorillas being hunted in Africa, and so on.
These chants also work well, of course, for your
human loved ones and for the perpetrators of cruelty as well.

*All I ask of you
is forever to remember me
as loving you.*

*Listen, listen, listen
to my heart song.
Listen, listen, listen
to my heart song.
I will never forget you
I will never forsake you* (x2)
A Jewish Chant

May the blessings of God rest upon you.
May God's peace abide with you.
May God's presence illuminate your heart
Now and forevermore.
A Sufi Chant

Chapter Nine

PRAYERS FOR SPECIFIC
ANIMAL NATIONS

THE HORSE NATIONS

First—A Little Horse Story

Heather, a person, and Smurf, her horse companion, were enjoying a ride on a path near some rocky cliffs when suddenly they found themselves in the middle of a rock slide. Rocks of every size were crashing down upon them. One hit Smurf's leg, causing him to fall. Heather was thrown off of Smurf's back. On the ground, rocks continued to fall around her. One landed on top of her, breaking her leg and pinning her. She couldn't move or go for help. Smurf limped over to Heather. Thinking quickly, as daylight was quickly fading, she tied her belt pack with a message in it to one of the stirrups and asked Smurf to go for help. Although the tendons in Smurf's leg were cut and he was bleeding badly, he hobbled a mile to the barn to save his friend with what the veterinarian called "pure guts and determination." Happily, both Heather and Smurf made a full recovery.[1]

A Prayer for All Horses
Oh, Heavenly Creator
Bringer of Love
Awaken me evermore to the truth of who I am—
A spirit who has come here to learn Love
Your will is compassion, joy, and freedom
for all horses everywhere.
I am your instrument
for your will to be done for them.
I ask for the blessings of peace and compassion
to go forth now to all horses on earth—
the horses forced to live on Premarin factory
    farms;
those in rodeos, circuses, races, movies;
those who suffer and die in abusive farms and
    slaughterhouses;
the wild horses being trapped and hunted;
and the happy horses in good homes or in
    sanctuaries.

I ask for the blessings of wisdom and compassion
to go forth now to all people who are

in any way causing harm to horses.
I ask for the blessings of grace and peace
to go forth now
to all people who are helping horses.
May compassion prevail for all horses everywhere.
And so it is.
Thank You, God.

Short Prayer for Horses

May compassion and love reign upon the earth
for all horses everywhere.

Meditation for Horses

Begin to breathe evenly and deeply. Feel peace at the
very center of your being. Think of a time in your life
when you were filled with joy and peace. Carry that
feeling with you as you go into this meditation. Sense
the presence of the Divine focusing with you on all the
horses of earth. There is a deep wisdom welling up in
the universe. Human beings are beginning to remember
that they and the horses are sacred beings, and that we
are all cosmically related to one another. Feel the powerful hope rising up—HOPE AND FAITH.

You are an emissary of God's Light. Your light
radiates out in great streams as it continually pours
through you. The more deeply you experience love and
compassion for the horses, the more cosmic energy
there is to power those beams of love to the horses

themselves. See your love embracing all the horses, soothing and encouraging them, letting them know, spirit to spirit, that they are not alone.

Now hold in prayerful thought the Premarin farm workers, the employees and owners of Wyeth-Ayerst Pharmaceutical Company*, the rodeo cowboys and their fans, the race horse and carriage horse people, and all the consumers who may know nothing at all about the cruelty behind the products and entertainment they are buying. These are all people who love and work hard and struggle and laugh and do their best to get through life. They are brothers and sisters of ours and fellow travelers on this journey to learn that love is the antidote to all our troubles. Allow Divine Love to rush into your heart as you contemplate your connection to all these sacred beings.

See your love for the horses and for the people, which comes from the Divine One, radiate out from your heart and mind along golden rays to their hearts and minds. This is the subtle movement of Love which, if directed with compassion and truth, is the most powerful force for good in the Universe.

And holding still, in quiet repose and peace, send this magnificent blessing of your Love to all those people working hard to improve laws, to educate people about who the horses are, to rescue horses from abuse and slaughter, and to maintain sanctuaries and adoption programs for horses.

Now as you come back to your daily life, bring your peace and your sense of knowing along with you. All is well, and all will be well.

Peace, Shanti, Shanti.

The Cow Nations

First—A Story about Mary the Cow

The Reverend O.F. Robertson lived with a cow named Mary. They had a very special friendship. As the Reverend got older, he became almost completely blind. Mary went everywhere with Reverend Robertson, nudging him with her nose or leading him. He was able to get around very well with her help. He did not train Mary to do this. She volunteered.[2]

A Prayer for All Cows

Dear Creator and Lover of all that is,
You have breathed precious life into us all.
Please bless and comfort our brother and
sister cows everywhere:
the cows suffering in feedlots,
in rodeos, on factory farms, in dairies,
at state fairs, auctions, and in slaughterhouses.
And bless the cows who have found happy homes.
For centuries they have lived,
faithfully serving humans
in spite of the suffering and death we have inflicted.

Help us to find ways to be your hands
and feet and voice.
Move through us as we offer ourselves
to be a channel of your undying Love.
Help us to know what to do each day
to help the cows. Shed Your brilliant light
of compassion upon each cow on earth
and welcome each one into your arms
as they pass from this earthly life.
I ask for the blessings of wisdom
and compassion to go forth now
to all people who are in any way
causing harm to cows.
I ask for the blessings of grace and peace
to go forth now to all people
who are helping cows.
May compassion prevail for all cows everywhere
Thank You, Great Spirit of us all.

A Short Prayer for Cows
May compassion and love reign upon the earth
for all cows everywhere.

Meditation for the Cows
Take some deep breaths, and begin to relax into your
place of peace deep within your soul. Place your hands
over your heart, and, as you do, call to mind the noble
cows all over the world. Allow your compassion and

love and God's compassion and love to build up in your heart as you focus your attention. Feel the energy of Divine Love filling your whole being. Now open your hands and feel all that love pouring forth from you. Feel God's Love pouring through you as you send it out to all the cows of earth wherever they may be. Imagine them receiving this love and comfort. Imagine that their fear level is declining; they breathe a little easier as they feel the Divine fountain of love pouring over them. This energy you feel is pure light and love, and it is real, and it is eternal. When you are sending this focused love energy to the cows, you are working with the Divine to bring light into the dark where it is so needed.

Now, once again place your hands over your heart. As you breathe, feel the love energy building. Now, open your hands wide and feel the love rushing through you and out to all people. Imagine this energy you're sending streaming out around the earth shining down in lovely light streams, bathing homes, restaurants, factory farms, dairies, slaughterhouses, rodeos, animal sanctuaries, humane societies, and cow rescuers with the golden light of love. Know that this energy is real and lasting and that others are joining with you in this blessed work of bringing true love here to earth.

Let us awaken ourselves and all the world to the Truth that Love is All There Is.

The Dog and Cat Nations

First—A Story about a Dog Named Barry

A little dog named Barry was born in 1800 and became the most famous of the St. Bernard dogs who lived and worked at the monastery high in a mountain pass between Switzerland and Italy. Since the eleventh century, when Saint Bernard founded the monastery, monks have maintained a hospice for mountain travelers and rescued many of them. In the 1600s the monks began training dogs, who came to be known as St. Bernards, to help them in their rescue efforts.

Barry himself saved more than forty people. One of them was a small boy who was traveling with his mother through the treacherous pass. An avalanche suddenly overtook them, sweeping his mother to her death. The little boy clung to life on the edge of a ravine. It was too steep for any of the monks to help him, but Barry crawled down the icy slope to the child. The child was unconscious, so Barry snuggled up to him and licked him until he woke up. The boy then held onto Barry's harness while the brave dog carefully made his way back up the treacherous rocks and ice.

In a French village, there stands a statue of Barry with the little boy riding on his back. Altogether St. Bernards have saved more than 2,500 people in that mountainous area.[3]

And a Little Story about Oscar the Cat

Oscar's human family had a new baby in the house. One day Oscar meowed loudly at the baby's mother, Kandy. When she didn't pay attention, Oscar jumped on the counter, but she just shooed him off. Finally, in desperation, Oscar bit Kandy's leg and began running around, meowing and gradually leading Kandy back to the baby's room. There Kandy found the baby—blue and not breathing. In the nick of time she picked up her baby, tapped him hard on the back, forcing out some food obstructing his airway, and revived him—all thanks to the quick thinking of Oscar the cat.[4]

A Prayer for Dogs and Cats

Oh, Loving Creator,
Make us instruments of Your mercy
and compassion.
Work through us to bring relief and liberation
to the dogs and cats of earth.
There are many who are happy,
and we send them love and blessings,
but there are many more who are suffering
in laboratories, puppy mills, and circuses;
in the entertainment, dog-fighting, and dog-racing
     industries;
in medical and veterinary schools;
and in homes where they are not loved
     or understood.

Spread your blanket of Love out
over the dogs and cats of earth,
Create in the humans of earth
new hearts of love for Your precious children.
We are all endowed by You with the power to
love and protect our cat and dog brothers
and sisters.
May this love, protection, and respect
be made manifest now.

Help us, dear Lord, to not give in to
discouragement
as we work, pray, teach, and sing this new song
of love for all beings.
Thank You for giving us this gift of
passionate love for all creation.
Thank you for this deep understanding
that You dwell in each of us
and in every sister and brother cat
and every sister and brother dog.
Our joy is in co-creating with You a world
where Love lives magnificently in every heart.
Give us the strength and inspiration
to teach love and to take powerful actions
to help bring compassion to earth.
I ask for the blessings of wisdom and compassion
to go forth now to all people who are
in any way causing harm to dogs or cats.

I ask for the blessings of grace and peace
to go forth now to all people
who are helping cats and dogs.
May compassion prevail
for dogs and cats everywhere.

A Short Prayer for All Cats and Dogs

May peace and compassion prevail on earth
for all cats and dogs.

Meditation for Dogs and Cats

In this time of meditation, be still and smile. Know that God's will is for Love to be the great motive behind every action. Know that God's will for you is to make love happen whenever and wherever you can. Breathe in God's Love for you and for all beings. That Love is in the air you breathe always. Let it flow through you as you breathe it in and breathe it out.

As you continue to breathe, begin to imagine a pure golden beam of light shining down upon you and flowing through you at the top of your head. Know that God is Love, and you are Love. Feel the molecules in your body vibrate to the rhythm of Divine Love. Know that each time you pray with such Love flowing freely from your heart, you help to awaken the world and to bring Heaven to earth. That is to say, you bring Love to earth, and where there is Love, fear and cruelty melt away.

Now, as you continue to be still and peaceful, call to mind the dogs and cats of earth. Feel the Love you have for them pouring out from your heart. At this moment, millions of dogs and cats are locked in tiny cages without the comfort of companionship or the freedom to run and play. Many of them are being injected with poisons, burned, cut open, mutilated, skinned for fur, separated from friends and children, and in general treated with no respect or love. Many of them will, nevertheless, lick the hands of those who abuse and kill them.

These mental pictures are terrible to contemplate, but know that you can continue to breathe deeply and remain centered in your divine heart. Allow yourself to let go of anger and outrage during these prayerful moments. The dogs and cats need us to bear witness to their suffering and at the same time to be pure channels for Divine Love so that it can flow in great energy waves from our hearts to theirs. See these dogs and cats receiving your loving attention. Do not doubt that this love you are giving to them is right now being felt by them. Your love is more real than anything else on earth, and it touches whomever you send it to instantaneously. See the dogs and cats feeling the comfort you are sending them. Breathe slowly and feel that awesome love pouring through you. And it is an awesome love, for if our hearts are broken open by the cruelty we see, imagine the tidal wave of compassion coming from the heart of God. Be with this flowing of love for as long as you wish.

Now, it is time to send this cosmic, unconditional love to the scientists, puppy mill owners, dog racers, dog

and cat fur traders, and all the others who engage in
animal cruelty. Be still in your heart and peaceful. Know
that they are all your brothers and sisters, and understand that they truly "know not what they do." They do
not understand the interrelatedness and sacred nature
of all life, including themselves and the dogs and cats.
Allow God's ever growing love for them to flow
through you like a mighty river. From your higher self
to their higher selves, spirit to spirit, mentally send this
message: "You are my sisters and brothers, and I am
sending you a gift on this wave of love energy. It is the
gift of seeing that God lives in every being. In your laboratory or puppy mill you are surrounded by God's
beautiful children. With this gift, you will find true
compassion for all beings, you will no longer wish to
harm even the tiniest creature, and through this new
love, you will find the greatest joy, for you will be in
harmony with God's love for all creation."

As you continue to send out this Divine Love energy, remember the millions of heroes who are daily
engaged in rescuing, rehabilitating, and caring for dogs
and cats, as well as those educating people about
respect for animals. They need your prayers for
strength, focus, and encouragement.

Now, when you are ready, begin to be aware of your
surroundings. And as you go about your daily activities,
remember—the work you have just done is real, and

many others are working with you. With the help of the Divine. which we truly have, we can do this.

And so it is.

Thank You, God!

THE FARM ANIMAL NATIONS

First—Two Stories about Chickens
and One Little Story about a Pig

A scientist wishing to study chicken behavior placed 21 guinea fowl eggs into a chicken's nest. He assumed the chicken was too stupid to realize the guineas were not her babies. Imagine his surprise when the mother chicken led her little adopted guineas not to the chicken feed, but rather to an ant nest where she showed them how to scratch the nest for pupae. Chickens do not eat ant pupae, but that's just the right food for guinea babies.

Another scientist placed duck eggs in a chicken's nest to see what she would do. To his amazement, she led her little ducklings to the water and encouraged them to swim.[5]

A young boy named Anthony swam out too far in a Texas lake. He was in danger of drowning, too tired to swim back. Suddenly, a little pig named Priscilla jumped into the water, swam to Anthony, and, as he held onto her, pulled him back to shore.[6]

A Prayer for All Farm Animals
Oh, precious Creator,
You who are in all the earth,
You who are in all your children,
You wash over us all
in heavenly torrents of Love.
Please lay Your Heavenly Hands in blessing
upon the billions of our brother and sister
pigs, sheep, chickens, geese, ducks, turkeys,
ostriches, emus, burros, mules, llamas,
and all other animals on factory farms and ranches,
where millions are being violently
abused and killed every day.

These blessed children of Yours
are all emissaries of peace.
They bring to us beauty in their sweet faces.
They bring to us peace in their gentle ways.
Help us, sweet Lord of Love,
to awaken ourselves and all humanity
to their suffering and their sacredness
and, thus, bring this long, sad, and bloody
era of human history to an end.
Help us to bring in the new era of *Homo ahimsa*!

Thank you, God, for helping us understand
that Your will and Your reality are that love and
compassion be expressed in all the earth

by all of us. Make us instruments of Your Love
and Mercy
for the animals of the farms and ranches.
Thank You, God.
Amen, We are One.

A Short Prayer for the Farm Animals
May peace and compassion prevail
for all farm animals everywhere on earth.

A Meditation for the Farm Animals

Begin to relax and take some deep breaths. Relax into
that place within you that is sublime, full of peace, full
of faith, full of joy. You are immersed in God's radiant
Love. Now, while you keep your heart centered in that
peace, call to mind the millions of farm animals who are
suffering today at the hands of humans. Each one is so
unique and beautiful. There are fathers, mothers, babies,
and children. They all have families and feelings. They
love and they cry, and most of all, they serve.

These animal nations have served humanity for centuries. They have shown us love, devotion, trust,
patience, and gentleness. They have been emissaries of
God's Love to us. They have laid down their lives for us
by the billions. It is time to give back to them the devotion they have given us. As you sit in meditation, be
aware of the great cosmic turning toward love. You are
part of this grand paradigm shift into reverence for all

life that is rising like a brilliant new sun. You are one of the movers and shakers making this sun rise.

Now, as you continue to breathe slowly and deeply, begin to look at the world from the point of view of your higher self, your eternal spirit. Feel yourself lifting up above the earth. Imagine yourself to be big enough to reach down to the earth from your place in the sky. Imagine reaching down to earth and laying your hand gently in a pasture full of sheep. Invite them all to step into your hand. They have no fear of you, and once they are all safely in your hand, you lift them up to your heart and sing to them. Ask God's blessing on each one of them, and listen to them as they tell you what is in their hearts. Then, set them gently back down in a beautiful green meadow where they can live in safety with their families and have plenty to eat.

In the same manner, imagine yourself as spirit lifting the roof off of a long factory chicken house and letting all the chickens out of their tiny cages. Let them all gather together in your hands. Listen to them clucking softly as you hold them close to your heart and whisper to them words of love and encouragement. Ask God to touch each tiny head and bless each chicken. Then, set them gently back down on earth in a safe place where they will not be harmed.

Now, as you continue to be in bliss high above the earth, see all the people who are engaged in farming, ranching, and slaughtering, and people who are buying meat and other body parts from them. They are doing what they think they have to do. Centuries of cultural programming have desensitized us to this escalating and unprecedented violence toward animals. From your vantage point of pure spirit, be aware that you are an instrument of peace and compassion. You have the power to send healing to all their hearts, so that if they choose to use the love you send, it is there for them. And while you are consciously aware of this river of Love pouring through you, think of the heroes who are rescuing farm animals, maintaining animal sanctuaries, and educating people about respect for life. Send them strength for the journey and faith in the power of Love to transform us all into compassionate caretakers of this sacred planet.

Continue to breathe peacefully, and when you are ready, come back to your daily activities, knowing that this peace is real and eternal, and goes with you wherever you go.

THE PRIMATE NATIONS

First—Two stories about Toto and David Greybeard
A gentleman by the name of Cherry Kearton was very sick with malaria. His friend and companion, a chimpanzee named Toto, took care of him. He brought him his medicine and books to read. He would figure out which book Cherry wanted by pointing to each book on the shelf until Cherry said "yes." Toto stayed by Cherry's side day and night until he recovered.[7]

Jane Goodall recalls a precious moment with David Greybeard, a chimpanzee. They were sitting together near some water. Jane spied a ripe fruit on the ground and held it out to David. He glanced at her and took the nut, but then dropped it, and gently took her hand. "He didn't want the nut but he understood my motivation, he knew I meant well. To this day, I remember the soft pressure of his fingers." Together Jane and David shared "a language bridging our two worlds."[8]

A Prayer for Primates

Oh sweet, nurturing Creator,
How blissful it is when our hearts awaken
to the mountains and oceans of your Love.
Make us instruments of
Your mercy and compassion
for all life is sacred
and in need of Divine Love.

Together we pray for all the primates of the world:
the gorillas, chimpanzees, monkeys, baboons,
orangutans, and all other primates.
Some are suffering in zoos,
circuses, and experimental laboratories.
Others are being hunted and killed or captured.
A few still live in their homelands with their families
but are in danger from hunters and habitat loss.
We know that You created them as

sacred, perfect, amazing beings,
divine expressions of You.
Thank You, God, for giving us this precious
journey on earth to share with them.
Make of us Your messengers of light,
that we may pray with all the power
You have given us for the highest good
for all members of the primate nations;
for their liberation from cages;
and for their freedom from suffering
at the hands of humans.
Help us, Lord, to hold the high watch
for them as Toto did for his friend.
Hold each one in Your loving arms this moment,
kiss their dear foreheads, and bless them
again and again with peace and faith
for a free and joyful future.
Thank You, God. Blessed be all our relations.

Meditation for the Primate Nations

Take a few moments to take some deep breaths and be
in that sacred place within that is always at peace. There
is a divine flame within you that no one can extinguish.
And no matter how deeply you delve into the shadows
of animal cruelty, that flame of love goes with you and
gives you the power and the passion to transform cruelty into mercy and rigid mindsets into awe and wonder.
How majestic are the great gorillas! How clever and lov-

ing are the chimpanzees! And all the monkeys—how
like us they are—cradling tiny babies, sitting side by
side in mutual friendship.

Now, as you relax and breathe peacefully, hold
your left hand cupped upward and your right hand
cupped downward. Pretend you are holding a ball of
light or energy between your hands. (In actuality you
are doing exactly that.) The left and right hands represent opposite poles, and yet together they form a perfect
whole. Hold your hands in this manner for a minute or
two and know that God is in the same way showing us
that all creation is already whole, healed, and one with
the Divine.

Breathe in the comfort of knowing that all is perfect
and whole for the primate nations, and that Love
always finds a way to bring truth to all matters, to
weave all opposites together. Now bring the whole and
perfect energy ball close to your mouth and breathe all
the love in your heart for the primates into that ball.
Watch the ball as you release it and allow it to float up
into the sky high above you and watch it send out millions of comforting beams of love. Watch as the beams
each make their way to every monkey, chimpanzee,
gorilla, and every other primate in the world. See them
all receiving the love, receiving the thought waves, and
stopping for a moment to savor your gift. Now instruct
this ball of yours to go into orbit around the earth and
to continue to emit these wondrous beams of love to all

primates from this moment on. As you gaze peacefully at your cosmic ball of love circling the earth and blessing all your primate friends, notice that the vibrations of love coming to each one of them creates a kind of energy field around each one. This energy field has the effect of blessing and softening the hearts of the hunters, experimenters, animal trainers, and others who are currently harming the primates. With enough of us holding this vision, sooner or later, Love will have its way. This energy field you have established also blesses and encourages all those working so hard to help our primate brothers and sisters. Because their hearts are so open, they will feel the energy.

Now, when you are ready to return to your daily activities, allow yourself to carry with you this profound sense of connectedness and wholeness that you have established with your love energy satellite continually orbiting the earth and sending your love and compassion to primates everywhere. You have done it. You are a divine instrument of peace. All the love you have sent out comes back to you multiplied.

And so it is. Thank You, Great Spirit.

A Short Prayer for the Primates

May peace and compassion prevail
for all primates everywhere on earth.

The Nations of the Waters

First—A Story about Filippo, a Dolphin

In August of 2000, Italian news reported that 14-year-old Davide Ceci, who did not know how to swim, fell from his parents' boat in the waters near Manfredonia, Italy. Davide's father did not immediately notice his son's disappearance. But Filippo, a wild dolphin who had attracted a lot of tourist attention in the area because of his friendly ways, noticed Davide's predicament immediately.

Filippo began pushing Davide up above the waves so he could breathe. When Davide realized Filippo was trying to save him, he grabbed hold of him and Filippo took him right to his parents' boat, staying with him until the boy's father could lift him back into the boat.[9]

A Prayer for Our Brothers and Sisters of the Waters

Oh Blessed Lover
of all the seas and lakes and rivers,
You who are the Holy Spring of Living Water
without which not one of us could live,
I give myself to You as Your instrument.
You who have made me a spirit being,
move through me and through all my thoughts.
I am Your willing vessel.
Let me carry Your love to the water nations,

to all the beings who live in the seas,
lakes, rivers, and creeks.
These sister and brother dolphins, whales,
seals, sharks, squids, all the fish and mollusks,
all the turtles and jellyfish, and all the
tiny one-celled people—
all are Your divine children,
all are members of my beloved family.
All are beings made of Your essence,
which is perfect Love and Joy.

There is the appearance of great suffering
among these, my precious relations.
Many are trapped and killed with nets,
hooks, harpoons, and guns.
Many others are harmed or killed by
trash and toxic chemicals made by humans.
But this appearance is a shadow over the Truth.

In Truth, I see Your perfection and
Your wholeness aligning perfectly
with all the water nations.
I see Your joy—the Truth of life—
manifesting in the hearts of all
and peace prevailing in every ocean
and in every drop of rain.
With joy and gratitude, I thank You, God.
Because You are All-Embracing Love

and Compassion, this work is done.
I let go of any doubts and
know within my God-self
Your truth is what is and nothing else.

And so ocean, lake, river, and creek nations—
receive this blessing of comfort and undying Love.
Peace and compassion prevail for all of you.
And so it is.
Thank You, Father-Mother God.

Short Prayer for the Water Nations
Peace and compassion prevails for
all beloved beings of the waters everywhere.

Meditation for the Water Nations
Sit quietly and breathe deeply as you enter your own
inner place of peace. Now cup your hands in front of
you. Imagine that the Creator is pouring into your
hands the tears of all the water people. When your cup
has been filled, sit in the silence, saying, "Thank you,
Universe, for this great privilege." Listen. Listen to the
beings of the great waters as they commune with you.
As you continue to hold their tears, your hands are
being anointed by the tears. It is your inspired compassion that brings you to this powerful moment. Give
thanks for this anointing as your hands are now purified and prepared to heal the beloved of the waters.

Hold your cup of tears now in your healing hands and observe in awe how Great Spirit, the Angelic Alchemist, poised above you, lets go a single drop of golden liquid Compassion. This drop falls in slow motion toward your cup and then enters into your cup of tears. Observe in awe as the new liquid in your cup, now golden, silver, shimmering in the sunlight becomes a warm, glowing ball of light.

As you continue to breathe peacefully, release your beautiful ball and watch it ascend into the blue sky. Observe as it takes its place in orbit around the earth. Observe it as it sends its beams of compassion, mercy, tenderness, and love to each dolphin, each whale, every seal, every swordfish, every lobster, every clam, every precious one of our brothers and sisters who make their home in the waters of earth.

As you think and believe, so it is.

Thank You, Lover of All Sacred Life.[10]

INSECTS AND OTHER TINY NATIONS

First—A Little Story about a Butterfly and Glistening Mirrors

Entomologist Harry Lange speaks of the day in 1941 that he dropped the last Xerces blue butterfly in his killing jar. "I could never have imagined it would be the last seen alive. I always thought there would be more. I was wrong."[11]

The little ones, according to Hildegard of Bingen, are "glittering, glistening mirrors of divinity." Meister Eckhart said, "If I spent enough time with the tiniest creature—even a caterpillar—I would never have to prepare a sermon. So full of God is every creature."

A Prayer for the Insects and All the Tiny Nations
Oh, Great Spirit, Holy One,
It is You who teaches me every day,
with each new lesson,
that I am one with You
and that You are in me and in every tiny creature,
even those we cannot see.
I know that I am Your beloved
and that You love all life through me.
I am a flute for Your love song to Life.
I choose now to make this music with You.
There is a great war being waged by humans
against the insects, worms, spiders, and all
the tiny living beings that bring life to the soil
and the air, the water and the woods.
And just as anger comes back to the angry one,
the insecticides and poisons are coming back
to the poisoners, hurting us and our children
and all of the earth and her children.

While the Light of Your great Love, like the sun,
has never ceased to shine, yet we humans

have created these dark shadows on the earth
through our ignorance and fear.
I now see with my true eyes the glory of
Your light shining on Your beloved little ones,
and in this great light, there is no poison gas,
no arrogant fist.
Instead, in this great light of Yours,
humans are awakened to the holiness
and the exquisite beauty and the intimate
connection we have with Your beloved little ones.

I know with profoundest joy in my heart
that Your perfect work is done
in each one of their lives.
I let go of any doubts and know that
You are—right now—blessing and loving
each one of them and bringing them
to their highest good.
And so it is!
Thank You, God.

A Short Prayer for the Insects and Other Tiny Nations

Peace and compassion prevails on earth
for our tiny brothers and sisters everywhere.

Meditation for the Little Ones

Begin to breathe deeply and evenly and travel gently to
your place of peace. Be there drinking in the perfection

and peace that surrounds you there. Breathe deeply, slowly, rhythmically. Float away from the earth so that you can see the whole planet from your place in the sky. Focus your thoughts on the insects and tiny beings of earth—the brown earthworms, the shiny black crickets, bright orange caterpillars, beetles, flies, mosquitoes, butterflies, and all the others. Some are free and busy doing their chores, taking care of their families, or perhaps playing in the wind. Others are being attacked by humans in various ways. They are being stomped, swatted, poisoned, captured and pulled apart. Their ant hills, hives, and other homes are being destroyed. They are being killed by the billions in a relentless war being waged by human beings against them.

Now, as you remain in your peaceful state of mind, observe the earth from your high vantage point. As it slowly revolves below you, notice that there is a dense, foggy substance over all the little ones who are being targeted for death. This is the energy of fear that you are able to see with your spiritual eyes, fear in the little ones and fear in the humans who want to kill them.

This energy is dense and can be drawn away. As you breathe gently and evenly, imagine a giant magnet high above the earth, not far from where you are. You have the power within you to activate this magnet. When you are ready, nod your head and signal the magnet to draw all the fear energy up to itself. Watch as all the dense, foggy fear energy is sucked toward the magnet. See it flying up from all parts of the globe, rushing toward this purifying magnet. As it collects there, it becomes denser and more packed together until it forms a small dense ball stuck to the magnet.

Now, as you continue to breathe evenly, focus your love energy on that little ball. Ask the Creator, the great Alchemist of Love, to transform the ball. Watch carefully and you will see one single drop of pure liquid Love magically come into view just above the ball. It drops onto the ball, and instantly the round, dense object is transformed into a bright, shimmering star.

After witnessing this miracle, turn your attention back to the little people on earth. Fly down from your place in the sky and find a little grassy place somewhere. Imagine some butterflies and bees, grasshoppers, spiders, moths, flies, and crickets all gathering around you and listening. Tell them that God loves them, that you love them, and that you and many others are teaching all the humans to love and respect them too. Tell them we can work together to bring peace to earth for all beings everywhere. Spend some time listening to them. They have much to teach us.

As you come back to your everyday life, carry this feeling of peace and intimate connection with you throughout your day.

Thank You, God!

ANIMAL NATIONS IN THE WILD PLACES

First—A Story about the Two Elk Who Saved Bryan
One September, fourteen-year-old Bryan Palmer went
hunting with his father and some other men in the High
Uintas Primitive Area in Utah. They were looking for
ruffed grouse to kill. Bryan left the group and, in the
process of following the call of a grouse, found himself
lost. As often happens in the mountains, it started to
rain, and the temperature dropped precipitously. Bryan
was dressed only in jeans, a T-shirt, and a light jacket.
Darkness began to fall. Bryan fired two shots, but no
one heard them over the mountain winds. Rain turned
to sleet, then snow.

Meanwhile, Bryan's father called in a rescue team.
Bryan stayed put and wondered how he would survive
the night with no warm clothing. As he sat under an
evergreen shivering, he suddenly heard loud snorting.
Frightened, he threw stones, hoping to frighten the animals away, but they didn't leave. Finally, he peered
through the branches and saw who it was—two female
elk. They came toward him and sniffed him. Then they
turned and left, but only temporarily. Bryan drifted off
to sleep, in the early stages of deadly hypothermia, but
he didn't die that night. When he awoke in the morning,
he found the two elk lying on either side of him keeping
him warm. Their backs were touching him and radiating their body heat.

Once he was awake, the protective elk got on their feet and trotted off. Shortly, Bryan was found, thanks to the dogs leading the search party. At first, no one believed the elk heroines saved Bryan's life, but the tracks and impressions in the snow verified the boy's story. Later Bryan made a shocking announcement to his father. He declared that he would never hunt again. "How can I possibly take the life of another wild animal after two wild animals saved my life?"[12]

And—A Story about Baby Beavers and the Trapper Who Loved Them

A trapper once found a mother beaver in one of his traps. She was dead, but her two babies were still alive. His wife Anahareo insisted that he bring the babies home and raise them. After a few weeks of being with the babies, the trapper vowed never to trap again. In his journal, he wrote, "Their almost childlike intimacies and murmurings of affection, their rollicking good fellowship not only with each other but ourselves, their keen awareness, their air of knowing what it was all about. . . . To kill such creatures seemed monstrous. I would do no more of it."[13]

A Prayer for the Wild Ones

Oh, Great Hunter of all Your lost sheep,
You who will hunt tirelessly
until all babes are safely in Your care,

You who have breathed the precious gift
of life into me and all my relations,
I understand that Your power to care
and to protect runs through me like a mighty river.
There are many, dear Lord, who have forgotten
how sacred Your children are,
and how much each one of them wants to live.
In their forgetting, they have come to think
that killing wild animals is not murder
but a sport or a way to make a living.
They are capturing animals for zoos and
for animal laboratories. They are killing them
for trophies and meat. And all of us
are living in homes and driving on highways
that have covered their homes with asphalt and
concrete.

Deep in our hearts, we know the truth.
Help us to look into the eyes of the deer,
the elk, the wild geese, the bears, the wolves.
Help us to awaken to our kinship with
all living beings. Help the animals
to know this deep connection too,
and let love and reverence spread
like the rosy, pink light of dawn.
In joy and thanksgiving, I greet this new day,
releasing all worries and knowing
that You can use my prayers

like sparks for flames
to set the world on fire with Love.
Thank You, Great Spirit,
for Your endless miracles revealing Truth.
And so it is.
Amen, Shanti, Shanti.

A Short Prayer for the Animals of the Wilderness

May peace and compassion prevail for all
the animal nations of the wilderness
everywhere on earth.

Meditation for the Animals of the Wilderness

Make yourself comfortable and begin to breathe evenly
and deeply, feel the peace of the loving universe washing
over you. Now imagine yourself floating gently up and
away from the earth. You may wish to fly with your
guardian angel or Jesus or Buddha or someone you trust
to guide you. Fly far enough out into the cosmos that
you can see the whole beautiful, blue-green planet that
we are privileged to call home. Now, from this spectacular vantage point, open your arms and drape a lovely,
pale green, misty cloud around Mother Earth.
Completely embrace her in this cloud.

Now smile as you watch millions of sparkling rain-
drops moistening the earth and filling the rivers and
streams. See the turkeys and geese, the deer and elk, the
elephants and gorillas, and all the animal nations of the

wild places drinking from these healing streams. Speak to them in a voice they all can hear. Tell them of your love and prayers and of the Divine plan for people to become compassionate and kind. Tell them of their sacredness and feel your heart connecting with their hearts. If you would like your guide to give them a message, allow time for that and listen and breathe and know. Know that all healing comes from love. If fear or angry thoughts arise, set them aside while you do this powerful, healing work. You are seeing the True Perfection of life and broadcasting it out into manifestation. As you do this, your thoughts of perfection are rippling out to the minds of all other beings. Now, take time to listen to them.

Be at peace. You are peace. You are beauty. You are love, and you are giving it forth to all the grateful animals, and they send you their light and love in return.

When you feel it is time to return to your everyday life, allow yourself to fly back to your place of peace. Feel the loving firmness of the earth beneath your feet. Embrace your guide who has accompanied you on this sacred journey. Know that the work you have done is completely real and absolutely effective. Thank you for doing this.

Thank You, God.

Chapter Ten

PRAYERS FOR SPECIFIC SITUATIONS, PRAYER LISTS, PLEDGES, AND WALKING MEDITATIONS

So many times, we see animals being cruelly transported in trucks on their way to slaughter. We pass by slaughterhouses, factory farms, feedlots. We see animals killed on the highways, hunters heading out in camouflage clothing, lobsters in tanks in the grocery stores, zoo animals pacing back and forth in their tiny cages, and the list goes on. Many times there is simply nothing we can do, at that moment in time, in the way of activism to help those animals. When that happens, prayer is a mighty action we can take for ourselves and for the animals, and it is a way to communicate with the animals, sending them comfort and love.

There are also situations, such as when we are preparing for a vigil, rescue, or march, that can be strongly enhanced by our prayers.

The prayers and thoughts don't have to be complicated or fit any certain formula. The Divine Love Energy is always right there within us and around us, ready to carry any messages we wish to the animals and others. Think about how rarely people have prayed for animals or even recognized that such an act would have any merit at all. When we send out positive thoughts of love and compassion to them, we are adding beautiful, new threads to the cosmic tapestry of life. There may be unprecedented cruelty on earth today, but there is also unprecedented compassion, and with each thought and prayer, we give it more substance, more reality, and more power.

Here are a few thoughts and prayers we can say for the animals that need us.

When You See Animals Being Transported in a Truck to Slaughter—A Prayer

Beloved brothers and sisters,
I am driving behind your truck,
and I witness your holocaust before my eyes.
I shudder at the mountainous cruelty
inflicted upon you by human beings.
Affirm with me and to the Divine
that Love is more powerful than all this,
and Love is now teaching everyone
that your life and all life is sacred.
You are emissaries of the True Light.
God is with you now; angels are with you.
When you go into the slaughterhouse,
march forward in peace and look into
the eyes of your killers with Divine Love.
Hold them in your gaze that they might
feel Its mighty power coming through you;

that they might be transformed
in heart, soul, and mind.
And know that you will soon be home
with your Creator, free, at peace,
where no more harm can come to you,
only everlasting love.
Know that I bear witness for you.
Know that I am present for you.
My heart and prayers go with you
forever and ever. Amen.

A Prayer to Say When Passing by
a Factory Chicken Farm

Oh, Holy Spirit of Comfort and Peace,
You know when the tiniest sparrow dies.
Thousands of innocent chickens have been
tortured and killed in this place.
My heart cries out in sorrow and shame
that we human beings have chosen
this ugly path of cruelty and pain.
Your heart of Love and Compassion
moves and lives in all of us.
Awaken all human hearts now, Lord,
to the truth and joy that Love is the only way.
Help me as I pray today to grow in kindness,
and show me how to illumine the hearts
of those who continue to harm the innocents.
I know that my desire helps to bring

Your Love here now. I see It covering
this place with Light and Love and Power.
This place and the people and chickens
in it are all transformed now by Your Presence.
We know that all the animals who have
died are with You now, living in peace,
finally resting in Your arms.
Dear chickens, hear my prayer.
I am holding the high watch for you.
I love you and bless you.
And so it is!
Thank You, Great Spirit.

**A Prayer to Say If You Are at an Amusement Park
and See Captive Dolphins**
Oh, sweet Lord of Joy and laughter,
You who are endlessly at play with us,
ever delighting in our smiles.
In our lack of understanding of the
true source of Bliss, we humans have
taken these dolphins from their homes
and families and forced them
to entertain us, thinking we would
find happiness in spite of their pain.
Restore us all, oh Fountain of True Bliss,
to the remembrance of our perfection
and of the holiness of all our relations.
Help all people to understand that true
bliss comes to the compassionate heart.

Dear dolphins, hear my prayers for you
and for all people that we will one day
live in peace together.
I know that in praying, I have helped to
set the vibration for you of the dolphin nations
to be free from our cruelty.

Today I dance with You, Creator of all,
and with all the dolphins,
and as we dance,
we draw the silver cord of compassion
all 'round the earth.
And so it is.
Thank you, Holy One-in-All.

**A Prayer to Say When Passing By Places where Fur,
Leather, Perfume, and Other Products Are Sold or
Made from the Bodies of Our Animal Friends**
Dear Lord of Deepest Care,
You who clothe us and feed us;
You who send us out to run and fly and swim
on hooves and wings and fins and feet;
You who hold us, each one, in Your arms
at close of day: I am Your child,
blessed beyond my own imaginings,
helpless before Your Love,
empowered by Your will for peace.
You have given me, by Your grace,

the true vision of Your perfect world.
By aligning my thoughts with Your vision,
perfect Love will come into view
as a lighthouse shines through the fog.
As I keep my thoughts sharp-focused
on Your light, I draw closer and closer,
and so recedes the fog of cruelty.

There are coyotes, wolves, dogs, cats,
beavers, minks, rabbits and many others,
all so beautifully clothed by You in skins
no artist could create in all the earth.
So lavish and mysterious are they that
people want them for themselves.
And You have endowed these animal children
with claws, scents, bones, tusks, and
other things all coveted by the humans.
So the killing and the torturing of our beloveds,
hunted, trapped, and caged, continues today.
And this is the appearance.
The truth, however, dear Lord of Love,
is Your Truth—higher, more real, not a
fading appearance, but an everlasting thing.

And so, I see Your hands and my hands
and the hands of all people laying blessings
upon these lovely beings, caressing their
soft fur and artful feathers and scales,

giving them care, attention, encouragement,
and lives of liberation and peace.
And as this vision of mine and many
others connects with Yours, Sweet Lord of Paradise,
I know that the work is done.
I let go of any doubts and believe that it is
God within us all that does the work.
Blessed be this work.
Thank You, Holy Mother, Nurturer of all life.

Meditation for All Our Relations Incarcerated in Experimental Labs

Breathe deeply and easily as you get into a comfortable seated position. Now go in your imagination to your place of peace, where your higher self dwells and where you are always full of joy. Breathe deeply. Listen. Be present in the moments as they pass. Now, hold out your arms just above your lap. Make a circle with them, fingers pointing toward fingers, but not quite touching. Imagine that within your round embrace you are comforting and communing with all the primates, rabbits, dogs, cats, mice, rats, guinea pigs, and others whose bodies are being used for painful experiments without regard for their dignity and well-being. See them all nestling into soft nests upon your lap and safe within your loving arms, completely at peace.

Whisper to them all, "We are all one. We are all connected and all journeying together in this great, sacred mystery of life toward Perfect Peace where our souls already dwell together. We are all one; we are all one. The Divine Perfection is present in us all. Together, with the help of God, the angels, and all those who live in the rhythm of Love, your nations shall be liberated and treated with the respect and dignity you have always deserved. Hold the vision with me, and do not lose hope." Now, as you gently lower your arms and settle the animals down onto the ground, observe them standing together with new hope in their eyes.

Breathe deeply and know with every part of you that you have truly communicated spirit to spirit with all these beautiful brothers and sisters. Be still and feel their gratitude, their willingness, and listen to their wisdom. Breathe, and as you exhale, see them raising their paws and feet and wings or nodding their heads in solidarity with you and in praise for the divine destiny toward which we are all walking together, our common destiny—Heaven on earth. Observe the Light of Love glowing from within and all around them and around you. Feel the peace, hear the great collective sigh of you all as you open to the truth that the coming liberation is real. The roots are already formed. The tiny seedlings are sprouting everywhere.

Now, as you begin to come back to your everyday activities, bid farewell to the animals, but know that this deep connection you have made goes with you always and can never be taken away.

Thank you, Great Spirit. Mitakuye Oyas'in.

Short Prayers to Use When You Hear about an
Animal Cruelty on the News

Often, we hear of atrocities toward animals that are geographically far away from us. Sometimes, the news is overwhelming. We cannot physically respond to every single event, of course, and sometimes we feel helpless and frustrated as the cruelties mount up. Not long ago, I received an e-mail about the bears in China who are kept in tiny cages their entire lives, unable to move, with catheters inserted into them to extract bile from their gallbladders. The pain is constant; their depression and loneliness unimaginable.[1]

When we receive communications regarding dogs or cats who have been tortured and killed, animals who need homes, bull fights in South America, gorillas being killed in Uganda, Congo, and Rwanda, their numbers reduced to 600 or less, and many other challenges, we feel the need to do something to make a difference. We can write letters and educate, and we can ask others to write. We can also pray and send positive thought and light. These prayers and thoughts are not small gifts.

Know that each animal for whom you pray is comforted by the love in your prayers and that each person who has hurt an animal is affected in a very real way by your prayers. Send out your light with confidence and faith that you are contributing to the uplifting of consciousness of humanity and all beings. Here are two prayers:

May You Be Free

May you be free from suffering.
May you be liberated.
May you realize universal compassion.
May you be healed.
May your angels watch over you always.
May the Great Spirit guide and comfort you
and bring you to your highest good.
If you have left your body,
may you follow the Light
and find eternal peace and joy
at home with the Creator of all that is.
And so it is.
Thank You, God.

Release

I hold in my hands your pain and your sadness.
Now I open my hands and release it all to God,
in faith that you will find the healing
and the perfect love
that you need right now.
And so it is.
Thank You, Holy Spirit of Unconditional Love.

A Memorial Prayer

Dear one, you have graced this earth
with your beautiful presence,
And now you are being called Home.
Look for the Light that will guide you there.

Your angels and guides and our Creator
await you with loving, open arms.
Father-Mother God, thank You for
caring for my sister (or brother)
in this life and in the next.
And thank You for the privilege
of being present at this holy transition.
Blessed be all my relations
And so it is.

PRAYER LISTS AND VISUALIZATIONS

Prayer lists are tools to help focus attention in meditation on certain individuals, groups, or conditions. The more you meditate with a prayer list, the more you bless each one on the list. It's especially powerful to carry your list with you as you go about your daily activities. That way, whenever you feel it in your pocket or think about it, you can energize it some more. Even without reading the entire list, you can still send blessings to everyone on it by simply spending a second or two with that intent or laying your hand upon it. The lists I have put together are not at all final, of course. Please feel free to add to them.

The visualization which precedes the lists can be used with any one of them to help you get into your place of peace and focus your intent. Or it can be used to send your love energy to the entire planet or to any

other list you may put together for yourself. It also
works well to begin with this visualization and then just
name various people, animals, and entities spontaneously as they come to mind.

Visualization to Expand Your Interior Love and Send It Out to All or to Those on Your List

I close my eyes and feel the love in me expand and
shine. All around my heart a golden glow lights up the
room where I sit. I focus my mind on Cosmic Oneness
and soon, within every beam of light that flows forth
from me, I see Unconditional Love, Divine Wisdom,
Holy Compassion, and Transcendent Inner Peace.
Powerful beams of light stream forth from me. I am
aware that I am transmitting Divine Light and Love
through me to everyone on my list. This Light that
flows from me and from millions of others today is
transforming the fear and violence in the world into
Endless, Perfect Love. There is an infinite supply of this
Love. It can never be depleted or lose its radiance and
power. I am an instrument of peace, and I am continually radiating a force field of love, comfort, and peace
out to all these beings. Together with them, I hold this
vision of peace and compassion encircling the earth for
all beings. Together we are all immersed in the Light of
the One Infinite Beingness.

And so it is. Thank You, God.

Prayer List of Animal Nations:
The Prayer Ark

Giraffes	Hippopotami	Zebras
Chimpanzees	Cobras	Rhinos
Wildebeests	Lions	Tigers
Jaguars	Cheetahs	Elephants
Camels	Lizards	Turtles
Yaks	Bears	Wolves
Eagles	Hawks	Owls
Elk	Horses	Cows
Foxes	Sheep	Pigs
Wild boars	Alligators	Crocodiles
Kangaroos	Dingoes	Ostriches
Emus	Donkeys	Mules
Chickadees	Sparrows	Finches
Parrots	Dogs	Cats
Salmon	Bass	Trout
Sharks	Rays	Hermit crabs
Anacondas	Fleas	Flies
Scorpions	Mosquitoes	Roaches
Clams	Eels	Jellyfish

(Add more names here.)

I love you. I bless you.
I bear witness for you. I am here for you.
And the Creator loves and blesses us all.

Meditation for Animal Advocacy Organizations

At this moment, I join my energy of love with all the compassion generated by the animal advocates around the world. I know that together we are creating a world where animals will be treated with respect and no longer harmed by humans. The more we do, the more the Universe rushes to aid us and the animals. I send blessings of love and light to these lightworkers:

Prayer List of Animal Advocacy Organizations[2]

- Americans for Medical Advancement, www.curedisease.com
- American Anti-Vivisection Society, www.aavs.org
- American Cetacean Society, www.acsonline.org
- American Vegan Society, www.americanvegan.org
- Animal Legal Defense Fund, www.aldf.org
- Animal Protection Institute, www.api4animals.org
- APASFA of Brazil, www.apasfa.org
- Assisi International Animal Institute, www.aiaianimal.org
- Association of Veterinarians for Animal Rights, www.avar.org
- Coalition to Abolish the Fur Trade, www.banfur.com
- Defenders of Wildlife, www.defenders.org
- Doris Day Animal League, www.ddal.org
- EarthSave International, www.earthsave.org
- Equine Advocates, www.equineadvocates.com

- Farm Animal Reform Movement, www.farmusa.org
- The Fund for Animals, www.fund.org
- Gorilla Foundation, www.gorilla.org
- Greenpeace, www.greenpeaceusa.org
- Humane Farming Association, www.hfa.org
- Humane Society of the United States, www.hsus.org
- In Defense of Animals, www.idausa.org
- International Fund for Animal Welfare, www.ifaw.org
- International Primate Protection League, www.ippl.org
- Jane Goodall Inst., www.janegoodall.org
- People for Animal Rights, www.parkc.org
- People for the Ethical Treatment of Animals, www.peta.org
- Physicians Committee for Responsible Medicine, www.pcrm.org
- Primate Freedom Project, www.primatefreedom.com
- Rainforest Action Network, www.ran.org
- Sea Shepherd Conservation Society, www.seashepherd.org
- SPEAK: Supporting and Promoting Ethics for the Animal Kingdom, www.speakingout.org
- United Animal Nations, www.uan.org
- United Poultry Concerns, www.upc-online.org

- Vegan Outreach, www.veganoutreach.org
- My local groups: Lawrence Humane Society, Animal Calling Association
- Your local groups
- Please add more, including peace and environmental groups.

Prayer List of Animal Sanctuaries[3]

- Animal Place, Vacaville, CA
- Best Friends Animal Sanctuary, Kanab, UT
- Black Beauty Ranch, Murchison, TX
- Blue Moon Animal Sanctuary, Lake Ozark, MO
- Candy Kitchen Rescue Ranch, Ramah, NM
- Cedarhill Animal Sanctuary, Caledonia, MS
- Compassion Seeds, Healdton, OK
- Cooper's Rock Mountain Lion Sanctuary, Bruceton Mills, WV
- Detroit Zoological Institute, Royal Oak, MI
- Dreamtime Sanctuary, Elgin, TX
- Elephant Sanctuary, Hohenwald, TN
- Farm Sanctuary, Watkins Glen, NY and Orland, CA
- For the Birds Rehabilitation Foundation, Phoenix, AZ
- Fund for Animals Rabbit Sanctuary, Simpsonville, SC
- Hacienda De Los Milagros, Chino Valley, AZ
- Maddie's Pet Adoption Center, San Francisco, CA
- Marine Mammal Center, Sausalito, CA

- Mindy's Memory, Newcastle, OK
- Mini-Pigs, Culpeper, VA
- Montana Large Animal Sanctuary, Polson, MT
- Mostly Monkeys Sanctuary, Ramona, CA
- Performing Animal Welfare Society, Galt, CA
- PIGS, a sanctuary, Charles Town, WV
- Poplar Spring Animal Sanctuary, Poolesville, MD
- Primarily Primates Sanctuary, San Antonio, TX
- Primate Rescue Center, Nicholasville, KY
- Project Hope Sanctuary, Duck Hill, MS
- Redwings Horse Sanctuary, Carmel, CA
- Sanaga-Yong Primate Rescue Center, Cameroon
- Southwest Wildlife Rehab., Scottsdale, AZ
- Texas Snow Monkey Sanctuary, Dilley, TX
- United Poultry Concerns, Machipongo, VA
- Wild Burro Rescue and Preservation Project, Onalaska, WA
- Wildcare Foundation, Noble, OK
- Wilderness Ranch Sanctuary for Farm Animals, Loveland, CO
- Wildlife Images, Merlin, OR
- Wildlife Rescue and Rehabilitation, Boerne, TX
- My local sanctuaries: Wildcare Wildlife Rehabilitation, Operation Wildlife
- Your local sanctuaries
- Please add more here.

Prayer List of Institutions of Animal Cruelty

For the people who work at these institutions and for the animals:

- Premarin farms where pregnant mares' urine is collected, most locations unknown, primarily found in North Dakota, Minnesota, Iowa, and Canada
- Wyeth-Ayerst and parent company American Home Products—producers of Premarin
- Proctor and Gamble labs where animal testing takes place. Locations are listed at www.pginfo.org.
- Charities that fund animal research: American Cancer Society, American Diabetes Association, American Heart Association, American Lung Association, American Red Cross, Epilepsy Foundation of America, Leukemia and Lymphoma Society of America, March of Dimes, National Multiple Sclerosis Society, Paralyzed Veterans of America, and others[4]
- Research centers that experiment on primates: Wisconsin Regional Primate Research Center, Tulane Regional Primate Research Center, California Regional Primate Research Center, Yerkes Regional Primate Research Center, and many others[5]
- Research centers that experiment on dogs, cats, rats, and many other animals. Most universities and chemical companies have such labs.
- All slaughterhouses. Some of the largest are in Texas and Kansas.

- All businesses involved in the fur trade: Fur farms, trappers, Burlington Coats, Saks Fifth Avenue, Macy's, Neiman Marcus, and Vogue magazine[6]
- All factory farms where animals are cruelly confined and suffer terribly, then are killed.
- All zoos, circuses, rodeos, horse and dog races, dog and cock fights, bull fights, aquariums, theme parks, and other places where animals are cruelly confined and/or trained under cruel conditions and treated with disrespect and disregard for their basic emotional, physical, social, and spiritual needs
- Medical schools that still use living animals in their curricula and labs: Universities of California (Irvine and San Diego), Illinois (Chicago and Urbana-Champaign), Miami, Mississippi, Rochester, Tennessee, Texas, Virginia and Wisconsin, Georgetown University, Howard University, Finch University of Health Sciences/The Chicago Medical School, Louisiana State University, Uniformed Services University of the Health Sciences, St. Louis University, Mount Sinai, New York Medical College, State University of New York Health Science Center, Case Western Reserve University, Northeastern Ohio Universities College of Medicine, Brown University, East Tennessee State University, Meharry Medical College, Texas A & M Health Science Center College of Medicine, Virginia Commonwealth University and Medical College of Wisconsin.[7]
- Please add more here as you discover them.

Vows, Pledges, and Commitments

These promises to oneself and/or to God represent a dedication to a certain action, service, or way of life.

The Animals Are Not Our Property Pledge
Originated by In Defense of Animals

Whereas, I believe that all animals deserve to be treated and respected as individuals with needs and interests of their own, and whereas I believe that animals are *not* commodities or property to be bought, sold, disposed of, or killed at an "owner's" whim, I hereby pledge to:

1) Adopt and rescue rather than buy or sell animals;
2) Live my life with an ethic of respect and consideration for all animals, rather than one of "ownership";
3. Represent myself as a guardian, caretaker, protector or friend rather than as an "owner" or "master."

Signed: _____
Address:_____

(If you wish to take this pledge and sign it, please make a copy and send it to In Defense of Animals, 131 Camino Alto, Mill Valley, CA 94941.)

I Promise

The Earth is my home,
a gift from the Creator of Love.
I promise to live in ways
that heal and honor the Earth.
I will love the land, the air,
the water, and all living creatures.
I promise to do my part to take care of the Earth
and to respect and protect from harm
all the animals of Earth.

Hindu Vow of Ahimsa

From me there shall come no injury, no pain, no suffering or destruction to life in any form. Even at the point of death, I will not hurt anyone, I will not injure anyone. I will not give pain or suffering to anyone. I will not harm anyone. I will not cause destruction or injury to anyone.[8]

Vow of Nonviolence

With God's help, I vow to practice nonviolence in the spirit and example of Jesus, St. Francis, and Gandhi:

- by seeking to be a peacemaker in all aspects of daily life.
- by accepting suffering rather than inflicting it.
- by refusing to retaliate against violence either in thought, word, or action.

- by using all nonviolent means to actively end war against people and animals and to end war within my own heart.
- by living a simple, vegan life and doing what ever I can to promote the emergence of *Homo ahimsa*.

Thank You, God, for Your Love and Grace, for I need them both in abundance to faithfully carry out my vow. Amen.

The Compassion Commitment

WE, the human residents of this beautiful, blue-green Planet Earth, do hereby declare that all of creation is sacred and interconnected. We know that all the stones, the mountains, the trees, the birds, the fish, the bears, the wind, the sun, all that is and we ourselves are worthy of awe and wonder. Whatever happens to one of us happens to us all. We understand that the Divine Creator is Love and exists in everything, everywhere, making every being an embodiment of Divine Love.

WE recognize that we can choose to evolve in the direction of full spiritual consciousness. We are spiritual beings blessed with eternal oneness, power, love, creativity, perfection, and divinity. We are rising from the status of competitive survivors to becoming gentle, compassionate caretakers of this miracle known as Planet Earth. We are expanding our circle of compassion to include all of God's creation, the entire family of earth.

WE hold the vision that, with God's unfailing Love and Assistance, we can create a world free of hunger and poverty and prejudice; a world free of war and violence against the earth, against animals, and against human beings; a world free of hatred and fear.

WE will use our power in our roles as parents, teachers, investors, consumers, voters, and active participants in life to promote harmlessness and compassion for all beings, peace and justice, and environmental sustainability, and to do our part to help life evolve to its full flowering in spiritual consciousness. In Mother Teresa's words, "Let us conquer the world with our love."

WE commit ourselves to hold this vision close to our hearts and to pray this prayer:

Oh, Divine One, we give thanks continually to You
for loving us so completely and, thereby,
showing us how to encircle the earth
with Love and Compassion as you encircle us.

May Love, Peace, and Compassion
for all Beings be expressed
everywhere on earth. Amen.[9]

Signed:_____

You may wish to copy and send this to the
Circle of Compassion Initiative
P.O. Box 1961, Lawrence, KS 66044

Vow of Compassion
(author unknown)
I shall be a believer of all that is Good in people and
    all that is deserving in animals.
I shall plead for their lives, campaign for their safe-
    ty, and uphold their right to a natural death.
I shall seek out the injured and the maimed, the
    unloved and the abandoned, and tend to them
    in their last days.
I shall not forget their place in the hierarchy of life,
    nor that we walk in each other's paths.
I shall bear witness to the wonder they bring into
    our lives, and to the beauty they bestow on our
    souls.
I shall restore their spirits when they arwaning,
    bind their wounds when they bleed, cradle
    them when they whimper, and comfort them
    when they mourn.

I shall be near them in their hour of greatest need—
a companion and a friend when their time has
come.

I shall watch over them and console them and ask
that the angels gather them in their arms.

From the creatures of the earth, I shall learn the
fruits of compassion and undying love and I
shall be called the beloved of God.

In their company, I shall indeed be blessed.

The New Ethics of *Homo Ahimsa*

We do not kill or maim animals for consumption,
clothing, sport, profit, or any other purpose.

We do not steal, pollute, or destroy their homes.

We do not use them in entertainment or experiments.

We do not steal their food or the food of their children, that is, their mothers' milk.

We do not confine them in cages, pools, or other
environments in which they cannot live according to their true nature.

We do not separate them from their families.

We do communicate with them whenever possible
in respectful ways. We apologize to them for the
ceaseless violence that has come to them at the
hands of humans. We pray for them. We thank
them, and we seek to understand them and to
listen respectfully to their wisdom.

We do assist them in any way necessary if our assistance is truly needed. Very often, they want to help us, and we gratefully acknowledge and receive their help.

We seek to assist ranchers, hunters, fishermen, scientists, and others, and we seek to assist all the animals who interact with those humans, in this gentle and divine transformation into a loving, compassionate world.

We live on this earth in friendship, peace, cooperation, respect, compassion, and love with our brothers and sisters, the animals, the humans, and all sacred creation.

WALKING PRAYERS

We are reciting our walking prayers when we are conscious of the sacredness of all life at the same time that we are engaged in daily living. In Eastern practice, this is called "mindfulness" and refers to being present in each moment and noticing the holiness of everything we see. It's so easy to forget who we are and what we're really doing here on earth when we're stuck in traffic or rushing around to get more work done than is humanly possible. It takes a lot of practice to be mindful in this way, but each time we behave in conscious ways, we send out vibrations of unconditional love into the universe, just as we do when we pray or hold positive visions.

Stopping for Turtles

For example, you might be driving down the highway when you suddenly see a turtle trying to cross the road. In mindfulness, you immediately see that this is a spiritual opportunity given to you and the turtle. When you stop and lift him out of harm's way, you save the life of a holy brother. In this one small act, you are saying to the universe, to God, to all of nature, and to yourself, "I care. I care for this tiny being who wants to live." You are praying with your hands and feet in recognition that all life is sacred and interconnected.

We are transformed by increments with each act of mercy and love. We are physically expressing the heart of God when we show such compassion. We may even enter into states of mystical bliss and deep inner peace through such acts, because, in doing them, we are participating in the Divine plan of reverence for all life. We feel God moving in our own hands when we save the little turtle, and we communicate, soul to soul, with him.

Roadkill Redemption

While we are on the road, more often than turtles, we all see many animals who have been killed by cars. In her article "Picking up Roadkill," Susan Tweit suggests a beautifully mindful act. When she sees an animal who has been killed, she stops, and, with the shovel she keeps in her car for such occasions, lifts the body off of the road. By doing this, she saves the lives of birds and others who might otherwise get hit themselves while eating the carrion. More than that, Susan is showing respect, honoring the body of the departed spirit, and giving it back to the earth. No one else can run over it again and further desecrate the body. It is now safe and ready to finish its earthly cycle in peace.[10]

As a child, I was always horrified by the dead animals on the roads. The longer the trip, the more we would see. It always hurt to see how utterly disregarded their bodies were. If they had been human bodies, all traffic would have stopped. Many rituals would have followed as the body was taken from road to burial plot. Yet for the animals, there was no sign of care or concern.

After I read Susan's article, I put a shovel in my car. I try to leave a little earlier for meetings now, just in case some dear relative of yours and mine has died on the road and needs a respectful ritual and a blessing to send his or her spirit on its way. Thus, he or she will know that someone was willing to bear witness to his or her death and deem it a significant event—a loss for us and a gain for heaven.

It's especially important to communicate with the spirit of the animal. Often, with people and animals, when a death is sudden and unexpected, the spirit is confused about what happened and needs guidance. It's very helpful to tell the spirit what has transpired and to help it to let go of earthly life and go toward the Light of Love.

OTHER WALKING PRAYERS

Veganism. Veganism is, of course, another walking prayer that helps remind us at every meal and every shopping trip that we are walking, eating, purchasing, and living in a sacred manner with respect for all beings.

Primate Freedom Tags. Another very profound act of prayer is to wear a Primate Freedom Tag. These look like dog tags but have the serial number of a particular primate and the name of the laboratory in which he or she is incarcerated. Wearing these tags is a constant reminder to the wearer to hold these primates in his or her heart and to bear witness to the suffering of all primates. Many people will ask you about the tag if you wear one, thus, giving you the opportunity to educate about the primate atrocities as well as raise consciousness about our kinship with all beings. See[11] for ordering information.

Silent Giving. Another form of walking prayer is known as silent giving. As you pass people, animals, trees, or any beings, silently send out love from your heart. Be aware that the Great Spirit is continually pouring Unconditional Love through you to everyone you see and through everyone else as well. However, it's up to us to take that vibratory energy and willingly project it out to others. Watch your thoughts, let judgments go, and just feel love, serenity, and joy radiating out to all who come near you.

It is easier to be in this giving vibratory state when you are silent. Once you begin to communicate verbally with others, it becomes more difficult. But the silent giving exercise helps us all to develop the ability so that we can use it when we are talking as well.

Walking Meditation. When you take a walk, pay attention to the present moment. Use all your senses to experience all the elements along the way. Repeating a sacred word or phrase as you walk may help you experience the string of holy moments even more deeply. This is walking in awe, wonder, and gratitude. As you breathe, feel your intimate connection with every being that breathes. The Source of All Life breathes through us and makes us all one.

In Closing

Improved laws for animals, boycotts, education, marches, and animal rescues are having huge impacts on the way people perceive and treat animals. The number of people willing to work for the liberation and protection of animals is steadily increasing. All these actions help to end specific abuses and, at the same time, help to address the root cause of animal cruelty, which is human fear, greed, and lust for power. They get to the root cause, because each act of compassion to animals, when it is witnessed, causes the witnesses to reassess their old assumptions about the animals, at least on a soul level, if not on a conscious level. When someone rescues a chicken, all who hear about it are moved. Some may laugh; some may cry; but all will be challenged to reconsider their old notions about chickens.

To save the animals, we humans have to save our own species from its own inner dark forces. This calls for a radical rising of human consciousness to a new level where our oneness with all life and the sacredness of all life is finally understood. We are in the very midst of this phenomenal emergence. We have left familiar shores; we are out on the choppy seas; but the fact that we have left the familiar behind demonstrates to those who are watching that we have faith that there is another shore. There is another paradigm—a higher ethic and spirituality by which we can all live, a consciousness of reverence for all life and a spiritual awareness of our oneness. Only with that ethic will we create a world at peace.

In this book, I am asking us to be a part of the spiritual movement to bring peace to earth for all beings. Prayers and positive thoughts are essential:

- for the animals,
- for the people and institutions who are harming them,

- for those who are rescuing and helping them,
- for the healing of the earth,
- and for all human beings to help us awaken to our divine, loving nature and leave our fears, ignorance, and violence behind.

Our prayers, positive thoughts, and spiritual faith are forces more real than anything else on this planet. By bringing the spiritual power of love to bear through prayer, we empower every single action taken for the animals. With our prayers, we can "get to people's hearts," as Jane Goodall asks us to do, remove the fears that lead to violence, and create an all-embracing circle of compassion. We are creating a new world while still living in this one. That's quite a project, but with focus, intention, and faith in the Unconditional Love that is the Creative Force of the Universe, we will accomplish miracles we haven't even imagined yet.

Norman Vincent Peale, the master of "positive thinking," says, "Have great hopes and dare to go all out for them. Have great dreams and dare to live them. Have tremendous expectations and believe in them."[12]

Let us hold the High Watch.
Let us believe we can bring Heaven to Earth.
When we put our determined wills together
with our Friends in High Places, we are
certain to succeed.

WORKS CITED

The Amicus Journal, published by Natural Resources Defense Council, 40 W. 20th St., New York, NY 10011, Vol. 20, No. 4, Winter, 1999.

"Animal Facts," Animal Protection Institute, P.O. Box 22505, Sacramento, CA, www.api4animals.org.

"Apology extended to Indians." Associated Press, 9-9-00, 5A.

Atmanandji. "A Five Point Plan for Jain Ecology." *Jain Digest,* Vol. 18, No. 1, January, 1991.

Berry, Thomas. *The Great Work: Our Way into the Future.* New York: Bell Tower, 2000.

Boff, Leonardo. *St. Francis: A Model for Human Liberation,* trans. John W. Diercksmeier. New York: Crossroad, 1982.

"Boycott Action News." Update in *Co-op America Quarterly,* No. 25, Fall, 1999.

Braden, Gregg. *The Isaiah Effect: Decoding the Lost Science of Prayer and Prophecy.* New York: Crown/Harmony, 2000.

Braden, Gregg. *Walking between the Worlds* (book and video). Bellevue, WA: Radio Bookstore Press, 1997.

Brown, Lester, "Fish Farming May Soon Overtake Cattle Ranching as a Food Source," Worldwatch Institute Issue Alert 9, October 3, 2000.

Callahan, Sharon. "The Care and Feeding of the Animal Soul." *Directions,* Spring, 1996, pp. 26, 27.

Carman, Judy. *Born to Be Blessed.* Pittsburgh: CeShore, 1999.

"Charities That Still Fund Animal Experiments," distributed by Physicians Committee for Responsible Medicine, 5100 Wisconsin Ave., N.W., Suite 404, Washington, D.C., 20016, www.pcrm.org.

Chopra, Deepak, M.D. *Ageless Body, Timeless Mind.* New York: Harmony Books, 1993.

"Church apologizes for sins of 500 years." *Lawrence Journal World,* 4-27-00. J-W Wire Reports.

"Concentrated animal-feeding operations," *Sierra: Exploring, Enjoying, and Protecting the Planet,* January/February, 2000.

Cunningham, Lawrence. *St. Francis of Assisi.* San Francisco: HarperSanFrancisco, 1989.

Davidson, Gordon. "Violence in America: Lessons in Causality." *Venture Inward,* July/August, 2000.

Davis, Karen. *Prisoned Chickens, Poisoned Eggs.* United Poultry Concerns, P.O. Box 59367, Potomac, MD, 20859.

Davis, Karen, and Nedim Buyukmihci, V.M.D. "Starving Hens for Profit Has Got to Stop." United Poultry Concerns, P.O. Box 59367, Potomac, MD, 20859.

Decade for a Culture of Peace and Nonviolence 2001–2010: A Resource Manual. Fellowship of Reconciliation, 521 N. Broadway, Nyack, NY 10960.

"Dolphin pushes boy back to his boat after fall," *Daily Record,* 8-29-00.

Dossey, Larry. *Prayer is Good Medicine: How to Reap the Healing Benefits of Prayer.* New York: HarperCollins, 1997.

Duda, Mark Damian. "Factors related to hunting and fishing participation in the U.S." *Fish and Wildlife Reference Service,* 1993.

Dyer, Wayne. *You'll See It When You Believe It: The Way to Your Personal Transformation.* New York: Avon Books, 1990.

Epes, Joseph, ed. *Black Elk: The Sacred Pipe.* New York: Penguin Books, 1987.

Estes, Clarissa Pinkola. *Women Who Run with the Wolves.* New York: Ballantine Books, 1992.

Ewing, Upton Clary. *The Prophet of the Dead Sea Scrolls: The Essenes and the Early Christians.* Joshua Tree, CA: Tree of Life Publications, 1994.

The FARM Report, Winter/Spring 2002. Farm Animal Reform Movement, P.O. Box 30654, Bethesda, MD 20824.

Foundation for Inner Peace. *Course in Miracles.* Farmingdale, NY: Coleman Graphics, 1975.

Fox, Matthew. *The Coming of the Cosmic Christ: The Healing of Mother Earth and the Birth of a Global Renaissance.* San Francisco: HarperSanFrancisco, 1988.

The Fund for Animals. "Hunting Fact Sheet #1." 200 W. 57th St., New York, NY.

Gandhi, Mohandas K. *Gandhi: An Autobiography: The Story of My Experiments with Truth.* Boston, MA: Beacon Press, 1957.

"Gandhi Speaks," booklet from Self Realization Fellowship, 3880 San Rafael Ave., Los Angeles, CA, 90065.

Gibran, Kahlil. *The Prophet.* 1923. Reprint, New York: Alfred A. Knopf, 1999.

Goodall, Jane. *Reason for Hope: A Spiritual Journey.* New York: Warner Books, 1999.

"Gorillas learn to wage peace against guerrillas," *Best Friends Magazine,* September/October, 1999.

"The Great Experiment II: Global Prayer Intended to Test Effect of Our Love on Planet Earth." *The Edge,* April, 2000.

"Great minds think alike," pamphlet distributed by In Defense of Animals, 131 Camino Alto, Ste. E, Mill Valley, CA 94941.

Hamilton, Joan. "All You Can Stomach?" *Sierra*, November/December, 1994, p. 38.

Hanh, Thich Nhat. *Call Me By My True Names: The Collected Poems of Thich Nhat Hanh*. Berkeley, CA: Parallax Press, 1993.

Harman, Willis, and Howard Rheingold. *Higher Creativity: Liberating the Unconscious for Breakthrough Insights*. Sausalito, CA: Institute of Noetic Sciences, 1984.

Hobe, Phyllis, ed. *Angels along the Way*. Carmel, NY: Guideposts Books, 2000, p. 43.

Holt, S., "The Food Resources of the Ocean," *Scientific American*, 221 (1969): 178–94.

Houston, Jean. *Jump Time: Shaping Your Future in a World of Radical Change*. New York: J.P. Tarcher, 2000.

Hubbard, Barbara Marx. *The Revelation: Our Crisis is a Birth*. Greenbrae, CA: Foundation for Conscious Evolution, 1993.

Hyland, J.R. "The Slaughter of the Innocent." *Humane Religion*, Vol. 2, No. 1, March/April, 1997.

In Defense of Animals Magazine, 131 Camino Alto, Mill Valley, CA, 94941, www.idausa.org.

Jones, Tim. *Dog Heroes*. Kenmore, WA: Epicenter Press, 1995.

Kansas City Interfaith Peace Alliance newsletter, third quarter, 2000.

Keyes, Ken. *The Hundredth Monkey*. Marina Del Rey, CA: DeVorss & Company, 1984.

King, Ursula. *Spirit of Fire: The Life and Vision of Teilhard de Chardin*. Maryknoll, NY: Orbis Books, 1996.

Laland, Stephanie. *Animal Angels*. New York: Conari Press, 1998.

Lehman, Louis. "Good Neighbor Policy." *Guideposts Magazine*, March, 1999.

Linzey, Andrew. *Animal Rites: Liturgies of Animal Care.*
London: SCM Press, 1999.

Listening to the Animals: To the Rescue. Carmel, NY:
Guideposts Books, 1999.

McIntosh, Phyllis, "Faith is Powerful Medicine," *Readers
Digest*, October, 1999.

Merton, Thomas. *No Man Is an Island.* London: Burns and
Oates, 1955.

Miner, Nancy. "Linked human and animal violence."
Speaking Out, Vol. 1, No. 3.

"Monkey See, Monkey Speak." *Venture Inward,* May/June,
2000.

"Monoculture: The Biological and Social Impacts."
WorldWatch, March/April, 1998, p. 39.

Neven, Tom. "A Doer of the Word." *Focus on the Family
with Dr. James Dobson*, Vol. 24, No. 9, September,
2000.

"Pathfinding Project." Institute of Noetic Sciences, 475 Gate
5 Rd., Suite 300, Sausalito, CA 94965,
www.noetic.org/pathfinding.

Plumwood, Val. "Being Prey." *Utne Reader*, July/August,
2000.

"Pope requests God's pardon for host of sins." Associated
Press, 3-13-00.

"Primate Experimentation: A National Disgrace," a booklet
produced by In Defense of Animals, Mill Valley, CA, in
partnership with the Coalition to End Primate
Experimentation, Washington, D.C.

Pritchard, Gene. "Out of the fog," *Guideposts*, January,
2000.

Ram Dass and Stephen Levine. *Grist for the Mill.* Unity
Press, Santa Cruz, CA, 1977.

Ray, Paul. "Cultural Creatives are from diverse subcultures
and change is multi-level." *Earthlight Magazine of
Spiritual Ecology*, Summer, 2000, Issue 38.

Roberts, Monty. "Monty Roberts: A Real Horse Whisperer." British Broadcasting Corporation, Worldwide Ltd., 1997.

Rosen, Steven. *Diet for Transcendence: Vegetarianism and the World Religions*. Badger, CA: Torchlight Publishing, Inc., 1997.

Sahajananda, Sri Swami, ed. *Heart of Compassion*. Divine Life Society of South Africa, Durban, South Africa: Sivananda Press, 1992

Schroeder, Mary E. and Dr. James Golden. *Science of Mind Practitioner Handbook*. Cottonwood, CA: Summerbreeze Publications, 1995.

Schul, Bill, Ph.D. *Life Song: In Harmony with All Creation*. Walpoint, NH: Stillpoint Publishing, 1994.

Schul, Bill, Ph.D. *Animal Immortality: Pets and Their Afterlife*. New York: Carroll and Graf Publishers, 1990.

Schweitzer, Albert. Nobel Peace Prize Address: "The Problem of Peace in the World Today." New York: Harper and Row, 1954.

Senate Report No. 307, 93rd Congress, 1st Session, U.S. Govt. Printing Office, 1973.

Shah, Pravin. "Organic Milk, Religious View, Usage of Dairy Products in Jain Temples." Jain Study Center of North Carolina, Cary, NC.

Shoss, Brenda. "Prayer for the Animals," pamphlet distributed by St. Louis Animal Rights Team, P.O. Box 28501, St. Louis, MO 63146.

Sivananda, Sri Swami. "Ahimsa." Divine Life Society Web site, www.SivanandaDishq.org.

"The Splitting of Giant Rock." *The Edge*, April, 2000.

Swearer, Donald K. "Buddhism and Ecology: Challenge and Promise." *Earth Ethics Journal*, Vol. 10, No. 1, Fall, 1998. Published by the Center for Respect for Life and Environment, 2100 L. Street, N.W., Washington, D.C. 20037.

Stallwood, Kim, ed. *The Animals' Agenda Directory of Organizations 2002–2003.* New York: Lantern Books, 2002.

Steinhart, Peter. "Cry the Ocean." *Mother Jones,* July 1994, p. 30.

TAOS Member List. *TAOS Horizons, Official Publication of the Association of Sanctuaries,* Vol. 5, Issue 3, Summer 2000.

Thurman, Robert. "How the Tibetans could save civilization." Institute of Noetic Sciences Pathfinding Project paper, Autumn, 1997.

Tweit, Susan. "Picking up Roadkill." *Earthlight: The Magazine of Spiritual Ecology,* Summer 2000, Issue 38.

Twyman, James. *Emissary of Light: A Vision of Peace.* New York: Time Warner Books, 1996.

"Vile bile farms release bears." *The Animals' Agenda,* Vol. 20, No. 5, September/October, 2000.

Walters, Mark Jerome. "Saying Goodbye: Mourning the loss of a species begins with remembering it." *National Wildlife Magazine,* December/January, 1999.

Washington, James Melvin, Martin Luther King, Jr., and Coretta Scott King. *I Have a Dream: Writings and Speeches That Changed the World.* San Francisco: Harper San Francisco, 1992.

"Why Vegan?" printed by Vegan Outreach, 10410 Forbes Rd., Pittsburgh, PA 15235.

"The world's benediction." *Creation Care: A Christian Environmental Quarterly,* 10 E. Lancaster Ave., Wynnewood, PA, Summer 2000, No. 10.

Wynne-Tyson, Jon. *Food for the Future: How World Hunger Could Be Ended by the Twenty-first Century.* Northamptonshire, England: Thorson's Publishing, 1988.

Yogananda, Paramahansa. *Autobiography of a Yogi.* Los Angeles, CA: Self-Realization Fellowship, 1946.

Yogananda, Paramahansa. "Undreamed of Possibilities,"
    booklet published by Self-Realization Fellowship, 1997.
Yogananda, Paramahansa. "Worldwide Prayer Circle,"
    booklet published by Self-Realization Fellowship, 1984.
Zukav, Gary. *Seat of the Soul.* New York: Simon and
    Schuster, 1989.

NOTES

*Publication details of works cited are found
above in the Bibliography.*

Introduction
1. See Shoss.

Chapter 1: Reverence for All Life
1. Mother Teresa, quoted in *Humane Religion,* Vol. 3, No.
   3, July/August, 1998. The statements in italics are well-
   known historical quotes, and can be found in Brenda
   Shoss's "Prayer for the Animals" (see Bibliography).
2. See "Why Vegan?"
3. Kowalski, Gary, quoted in *Humane Religion*, Vol. 3,
   No. 2, May/June, 1998.
4. Laurens van der Post, quoted in Linzey.
5. See "Gorillas . . ."
6. See Davidson, p. 27.
7. See Ram Dass, p. 81.
8. See Kansas City, p. 3.
9. See Miner.
10. People for the Ethical Treatment of Animals, "School
    shootings linked by animal cruelty," 1999. See
    www.peta.org/cmp/viol.html.
11. Ibid.
12. Mead, Margaret, "Cultural Factors in the Cause and
    Prevention of Pathological Homicide," *Bulletin in the*

Menninger Clinic, No. 28 (1964), quoted in People for the Ethical Treatment of Animals, "Animal abuse and human abuse: partners in crime," http://www.peta.org/mc/facts/ fsc24.html.

13. "Parallels of Oppression," *In Defense of Animals* magazine, Vol. 3, Spring, 2000.
14. See Estes.
15. See Schul, p. 64.
16. See Laland.
17. Carl Sagan, quoted in "Great minds . . ."
18. See "Primate Experimentation . . ."
19. V.A. Holmes-Gore, quoted in *Humane Religion,* Vol 3, No. 3, July/August, 1998.
20. See Laland.
21. "Premarin: A prescription for cruelty," People for the Ethical Treatment of Animals, Factsheet #15.
22. See Roberts.
23. See Yogananda, p. 9.

Chapter 2: A New Humanity Coming into Form

1. See Harman.
2. See Twyman.
3. See Braden.
4. See Houston.
5. See Hubbard.
6. See Fox.
7. See Zukav.
8. See Yogananda, "Undreamed of Possibilities," p. 28.
9. See "Gandhi Speaks."
10. See King.
11. See Carman.
12. See Goodall.
13. See Berry.
14. See Ray.
15. See "The Splitting . . . "
16. See "Pope . . . "

17. See "Church . . . "
18. See "Apology . . . "
19. United Religions Initiative, P.O. Box 29242, San Francisco, CA, 94129-0242, www.uri.org.
20. Norman Cousins, quoted in "Why Vegan?"
21. Leonardo da Vinci, quoted in "Great minds . . ."
22. See Hobe.
23. T. L. Vaswami, quoted in Sahajananda, p. 227.
24. Henry David Thoreau, quoted in "Why Vegan?"
25. See Schweitzer.
26. Charles Darwin, quoted in "Great minds . . ."
27. Gandhi, quoted in "Great minds . . ."
28. Thomas Edison, quoted in "Why Vegan?"
29. See Berry.
30. See Schul, *Animal Immortality,* p. 212.
31. Christian Science Sentinel, 1987, quoted in *Humane Religion,* Vol. 3, No. 2, May/June, 1998, p. 8.
32. Gorilla Foundation, Box 620530, Woodside, CA 94062-0530, www.koko.org.
33. See "Monkey . . . " p. 9.
34. See Pritchard.
35. See Laland, pp. 25–26.
36. See Schul, *Life Song,* p. 94.
37. Ibid.
38. Mark Twain, Notebook, 1894.
39. Henry Ward Beecher, quoted in *Humane Religion,* Vol. 3, No. 2, May/June, 1998, p. 16.
40. See Callahan, pp. 26, 27.
41. See Gandhi, p. 430.
42. See Thurman.
43. See Gibran.

Chapter 3: Divine Will

1. See Washington.
2. See King.

3. Fyodor Mikhail Dostoevsky, *The Brothers Karamazov,* tr. David Magarshack, New York: Penguin Books, 1969, quoted in Linzey.

4. Leadbeater, C.W., *The Collected Works*, quoted in *Humane Religion*, Vol. 3, No. 3, July/August, 1998, p. 23.

5. See *Amicus Journal*, p. 16.

6. See Yogananda, *Autobiography of a Yogi.*

7. Calvin DeWitt, in *Green Cross* magazine, Vol. 4, No.1, Winter, 1998, p.9.

8. See Walters, p. 37.

9. See Laland, p. 37.

10. Ibid., pp. 36, 37.

11. See Hanh, from the poem "Walking Meditation."

12. See Merton, p. 16.

13. Leo Tolstoy, quoted in "Compassionate Quotes," pamphlet distributed by Jain Study Center of North Carolina (Raleigh), 509 Carriage Wood Circle, Raleigh, NC 27606, http://www.jainism.org.

14. See Ram Dass, p. 96.

Chapter 4: Sacrifice, Crucifixion, and Resurrection

1. See Gandhi, p. 235.

2. See Cunningham, p. 62.

3. See Hyland.

4. Carl A. Skriver, quoted in *Humane Religion*, Vol. 1, No. 6, January/February 1997.

5. See Neven.

6. See Gandhi.

7. See Cunningham.

8. See FARM Report.

9. See Brown.

10. See "Monoculture . . ." and Steinhart.

11. See Hamilton.

12. See Holt.

13. See "Animal Facts."

14. See "Concentrated animal-feeding . . . " p. 49.
15. "Vegetarianism: Eating for Life," People for the Ethical Treatment of Animals, Factsheet #5.
16. Ibid.
17. Ibid.
18. See The Fund for Animals.
19. See *Senate Report No. 307.*
20. See The Fund for Animals.
21. See Duda. Some facts were compiled by The Fund for Animals.
22. See Davis.
23. See "Animal Facts."
24. Ibid.
25. Ibid.
26. Ibid.
27. See www.premarinfree.com.
28. See "Why Vegan?"
29. See Wynne-Tyson.
30. Yogananda, "Worldwide Prayer Circle," p. 11.
31. St. Bonaventure, quoted in Linzey, p. 147.
32. Shik Po Chih, quoted in Shoss.
33. See Linzey, p. 67.
34. Ibid., p. 96.
35. Christiaan Barnard, quoted in Shoss.
36. Mark Twain, quoted in Shoss.
37. Andrew Linzey, quoted in *Humane Religion,* Vol. 3, No. 2, May/June 1998, p. 15.
38. Callahan, pp. 7, 8.

Chapter Five: *Homo Ahimsa*
1. See Sivananda.
2. See Shah.
3. See Atmanandji.
4. Humphrey Primatt, "Duty of Mercy," quoted in *Humane Religion,* Vol. 3, No. 2, May/June, 1998.
5. John Woolman, quoted in Linzey, p. 142.

6. Plutarch, quoted in "Why Vegan?"
7. See Shoss.
8. Sivananda, pp. 2, 4.
9. Gandhi, p. 504.
10. See Epes.
11. See Gandhi.
12. Gandhi, p. 321.
13. Ibid., p. 323.
14. Ibid., p. 449.
15. See Washington.
16. Ibid.
17. Sivananda, p. 2.
18. Ibid.
19. See Lehman.
20. Sivananda, p. 2.
21. Gandhi, p. 349.
22. Ibid., pp. 504, 505, 449.
23. See Ewing.
24. Cunningham, p. 61.
25. Ibid., p. 11, 63.
26. See Shoss.
27. Cunningham, pp. 65–66.
28. Boff, p. 72.
29. Ibid., p. 96.
30. Ibid., p. 99.
31. See Foundation for Inner Peace.
32. Basil Wrighton, quoted in *Humane Religion*, Volume 3, No. 2, May/June, 1998, p. 16.
33. Isaac Bashevis Singer, quoted in Rosen.
34. "Why Vegan?" p. 6.
35. McGill, Henry C., et al. "Association of Coronary Heart Disease Risk Factors with Microscopic Qualities of Coronary Atherosclerosis in Youth." *Circulation* 2000; 102: 374.
36. Wynne-Tyson, reference to Korean study on page 72.
37. Ralph Waldo Emerson, quoted in "Why Vegan?"

38. Wynne-Tyson, p. 144.
39. Plumwood, pp. 56–61.
40. Edgar Kupfer, quoted in Laland, p. 6.
41. Ramalinga description found at www.vallalar.org.
42. Fillmore, Charles, quoted in *Humane Religion,* Vol. 3, No. 3, July/August, 1998.
43. Humphrey Primatt, quoted by J.R. Hyland in "Animal and Human Companions," *Humane Religion,* Vol. 2, No. 4, September/October, 1997.

Chapter 6: Transformative Power of Positive Thought and Prayer
1. Yogananda, "Worldwide Prayer Circle," p. 6.
2. Abraham Joshua Heschel, quoted in *Decade for a Culture . . .*
3. See Dyer.
4. See Schroeder, p. 17.
5. Gandhi, p. 72.
6. Gandhi in "Gandhi Speaks."
7. See Keyes.
8. See McIntosh.
9. See Dossey.
10. See McIntosh.
11. See Braden, *The Isaiah Effect.*
12. See "The world's benediction."
13. Linzey, p. 1.
14. Ibid., p. 3.

Chapter 7: Prayer Power in Action
1. Boff, pp. 48, 49.
2. Yogananda, "Worldwide Prayer Circle," p. 24.
3. See "Pathfinding Project."
4. Yogananda, p. 24.
5. Gandhi, p. 190.
6. Alcoholics Anonymous, *Twelve Steps and Twelve Traditions.* Alcoholics Anonymous World Services, 1996.

7. See Ram Dass.
8. See Chopra.

Chapter 8: General Prayers

1. Facts about Coleridge's poem found in *Humane Religion*, pp.15–20, Vol. 1, No. 6, January/February 1997.
2. This is part of a "Service for Animal Welfare" written by Andrew Linzey, who holds the world's first post in theology and animal welfare. See Linzey, pp. 34, 35.
3. Linzey, p. 105.
4. See "The Great Experiment." For more information on the experiment, go to www.greggbraden.com. For information about the phrase "May Peace Prevail on Earth," contact the World Peace Prayer Society at 800 Third Ave., 37th Floor, NY, NY 10022 or peacepal@world-peace.org.
5. Amerson, Edward. Prayer written for this book. Copyright 2000 by Edward Amerson. Amerson is the author of *Sing with Wolves* and *On Silent Wings*.
6. St. Basil quoted in *Humane Religion*, Vol.1, No. 6, January/February, 1997, p. 3.
7. See Swearer.
8. This Buddhist prayer was offered in Assisi, Italy, in 1986, at the Day of Prayer for World Peace. quoted in Twyman, p. 21.
9. Albert Schweitzer, *Memoirs of Childhood and Youth* (Syracuse, NY: Syracuse University Press, 1997, p. 37), quoted in Linzey p. 145.
10. This Jain prayer was also offered in Assisi, Italy, in 1986, and is quoted in Twyman, p. 61.

Chapter 9: Prayers for Specific Animal Nations

1. Zullo, Allan, "The Little Horse That Could," *Listening to the Animals: To the Rescue*, pp. 34–43.
2. Laland, p. 49.

3. See Jones.
4. Laland, p. 166.
5. Ibid., p. 75.
6. Ibid., p. 88.
7. Ibid, p. 6.
8. See Goodall.
9. See "Dolphin pushes boy . . . "
10. This visualization and the previous one are adapted from suggestions in a handout entitled "Earth Spirituality Practice for Everyday Life." I would like to give credit to the author for these beautiful ideas, but there was no name on the paper.
11. Lange, Harry, quoted in Walters, p. 37.
12. *Listening to the Animals: To the Rescue,* pp. 136–146.
13. Laland, p. 8.

Chapter 10: Prayers for Specific Situations . . .
1. "Vile bile farms . . . " p. 8. The article states that 500 bears are being rescued, but there are an estimated 7,000 in the tiny cages.
2. See Stallwood for a comprehensive list of animal advocacy organizations in the United States and around the world.
3. Organizations from the TAOS Member List.
4. For a complete list, see "Charities that Still Fund . . ."
5. For a complete list go to www.primatefreedom.com/researchcenters, maintained by the Primate Freedom Project.
6. See "Boycott Action News."
7. This list was supplied by the Physicians Committee for Responsible Medicine, which maintains and updates the list at: www.pcrm.org/resch/meded/ethics_medlab_list.html.
8. Sivananda, "Ahimsa," p. 6.
9. See Carman.
10. See Tweit.

11. Primate Freedom Tags can be ordered from the Primate Freedom Project at www.primatefreedom.com, or send $10.00 to Freedom Tags, 54 Gray Lawn Ave., Petaluma, CA 94952. Specify whether you want a necklace or bracelet.
12. Norman Vincent Peale, *Guideposts*, November, 2000, p. 60.

The Dominion of Love
Animal Rights According to the Bible
NORM PHELPS

"After decades of neglect, churches are beginning to take the issue of justice to animals seriously. Many books have influenced this change, and *The Dominion of Love* is an insightful, judicious, and inspiring contribution to this growing library."—The Rev. Dr. **Andrew Linzey**, *Oxford University*; author, *Animal Theology*

Eternal Treblinka
Our Treatment of Animals and the Holocaust
CHARLES PATTERSON, PH.D.
Foreword by Lucy Rosen Kaplan, Esq.

"Grim, compelling."—*Midwest Book Review*

God's Covenant with Animals
A Biblical Basis for the Humane Treatment of All Creatures
J. R. HYLAND

"[Hyland] speaks with great authority, combining scholarship and passion with a prophetic voice."
—**Stephen H. Webb**, author of *On God and Dogs*

The Inner Art Trilogy
Spiritual Practices for Body and Soul
CAROL J. ADAMS
Including:
The Inner Art of Vegetarianism
The Inner Art of Vegetarianism Workbook
Meditations on the Inner Art of Vegetarianism

An exploration of the inner life of vegetarianism and the outer life of compassion in action.

More Than a Meal
The Turkey in Myth, History, Ritual, and Tradition
KAREN DAVIS, PH.D.

"Shines a new light on the unfortunate, much-maligned bird."—Peter Singer

The PETA Celebrity Cookbook
Delicious Vegetarian Recipes from Your Favorite Stars

Celebrities such as Alec Baldwin, Russell Simmons, Alicia Silverstone and Paul McCartney reveal their favorite vegetarian recipes.

Pet Loss
JULIA HARRIS

Insightfully and helpfully, Julia Harris guides grieving pet owners through the many emotional reactions and responses to the loss of a pet.

A Primer on Animal Rights
*Leading Experts Write about Animal Cruelty
and Exploitation*
KIM STALLWOOD

Articles that document how animals are cruelly mistreated
and commercially exploited for profit.

Stories Rabbits Tell
*A Natural and Cultural History of a Misunderstood
Creature*
SUSAN E. DAVIS AND MARGO DEMELLO

"Stories Rabbits Tell explains exactly why I will always have
rabbits in my life—they're playful, quick, frisky, sexy, clever,
smart, childish, fearless, innocent, interesting, and inquisi-
tive. This book says it all—it's inspiring, like rabbits are."
　　　　　　　　　　　—Amy Sedaris, comedian and author

Strolling with Our Kin
Speaking for and Respecting Voiceless Animals
MARC BEKOFF
Foreword by Jane Goodall

"A major inspiration."—*Journal of Agricultural and
Environmental Sciences*

The Vegan Diet as Chronic Disease Prevention
Evidence Supporting the New Four Food Groups
KERRIE K. SAUNDERS, PH.D.

"Kerrie Saunders' new book is a wonderfully practical guide to using nutrition to prevent and treat a huge range of health problems. Knowledgeably and clearly written, this book will be a useful resource for many years to come."
—Neal D. Barnard, M.D.

To ORDER:
Call 1.800.856.8664 or visit www.lanternbooks.com